MW00426202

TO:

Brayden

FROM:

The Griffiths

God bless you!

DATE:

10·22·2022

Published by Christian Art Publishers
PO Box 1599, Vereeniging, 1930, RSA

First edition 2019

Designed by Christian Art Publishers

Images used under license from Shutterstock.com

Printed in China

ISBN 978-1-4321-2995-8 (Faux Leather)
ISBN 978-1-4321-3025-1 (Genuine Leather)

21 22 23 24 25 26 27 28 29 30 – 13 12 11 10 9 8 7 6 5 4

PROMISES FROM GOD FOR *Every Man*

CONTENTS PAGE

God's way
IS PERFECT.
ALL THE
LORD'S PROMISES
prove true.
He is
A SHIELD
FOR ALL WHO
look to Him for
PROTECTION.

Psalm 18:30

GOD KEEPS HIS PROMISES

God truly is righteous and holy and He will never deceive you. He is gracious and good and will never forget you. He is eternal and true and He will never change.

Nothing is impossible for Him because He is omnipotent. Whatever He promises, He can and will do!

Loving Father, thank You that I can depend on Your promises forever and into eternity.

AMEN.

The Lord's promises are pure, like silver refined in a furnace, purified seven times over.

PSALM 12:6 NLT

The heavens praise Your wonders, Lord, Your faithfulness too, in the assembly of the holy ones.

PSALM 89:5 NIV

The Lord will cover you with His feathers. He will shelter you with His wings. His faithful promises are your armor and protection.

PSALM 91:4 NLT

Know therefore that the Lord your God is God; He is the faithful God, keeping His covenant of love to a thousand generations of those who love Him and keep His commandments.

DEUTERONOMY 7:9 NIV

The Lord always keeps His promises; He is gracious in all He does.

PSALM 145:13 NLT

If we are faithless, He remains faithful; He cannot deny Himself.

2 TIMOTHY 2:13 NKJV

The Scriptures tell us, "Anyone who trusts in Him will never be disgraced."

ROMANS 10:11 NLT

Sovereign Lord, You are God! Your covenant is trustworthy.

2 SAMUEL 7:28 NIV

Your decrees are very trustworthy; holiness befits Your house, O LORD, forevermore.

PSALM 93:5 ESV

God is faithful, who has called you into fellowship with His Son, Jesus Christ our Lord.

---

1 CORINTHIANS 1:9 NIV

Steadfast love will be built up forever; in the heavens You will establish Your faithfulness.

PSALM 89:2 ESV

Your faithfulness extends to every generation, as enduring as the earth You created.

PSALM 119:90 NLT

He is the Maker of heaven and earth, the sea, and everything in them – He remains faithful forever.

PSALM 146:6 NIV

I will sing of the LORD's unfailing love forever! Young and old will hear of Your faithfulness.

PSALM 89:1 NLT

The LORD will work out His plans for my life – for Your faithful love, O LORD, endures forever.

PSALM 138:8 NLT

God is not a man, that He should lie, nor a son of man, that He should repent. Has He said, and will He not do? Or has He spoken, and will He not make it good?

NUMBERS 23:19 NKJV

BLESSED
IS THE MAN
WHO TRUSTS
IN THE LORD,
AND WHOSE
HOPE
IS THE LORD.

JEREMIAH 17:7

TRUST
IN THE LORD

Through the ages, people have had to deal with dangers and testing in a variety of forms. Today our faith is still tested. It might be through financial difficulties, sickness or some kind of personal setback. Whatever your situation, always remember that God is with you to support you and to carry you through your time of difficulty.

Cling to the presence of the Living Christ in your life. He will inspire you to a life of trust and firm faith in all circumstances.

My Savior, in You I discover unending joy, love and true life. I thank You for this.

AMEN.

Blessed is the man who makes the Lord his trust.

PSALM 40:4 ESV

The fear of man brings a snare, but whoever trusts in the Lord shall be safe.

PROVERBS 29:25 NKJV

Anyone who trusts in Him will never be disgraced.

ROMANS 10:11 NLT

Trust in the Lord with all your heart, and lean not on your own understanding; in all your ways acknowledge Him, and He shall direct your paths.

PROVERBS 3:5-6 NKJV

Those who listen to instruction will prosper; those who trust the LORD will be joyful.

PROVERBS 16:20 NLT

Trust in Him at all times, O people; pour out your heart before Him; God is a refuge for us.

PSALM 62:8 ESV

The LORD is good, a refuge in times of trouble.
He cares for those who trust in Him.

NAHUM 1:7 NIV

Trust in the LORD always, for the LORD God is the eternal Rock.

ISAIAH 26:4 NLT

Let the morning bring me word of Your unfailing love, for I have put my trust in You.

PSALM 143:8 NIV

"I am the LORD, and I do not change."

MALACHI 3:6 NLT

In God I have put my trust; I will not be afraid. What can man do to me?

PSALM 56:11 NKJV

"Do not let your hearts be troubled. You believe in God; believe also in Me."

JOHN 14:1 NIV

Those who know Your name trust in You, for You, LORD, have never forsaken those who seek You.

PSALM 9:10 NIV

If we are faithful to the end, trusting God just as firmly as when we first believed, we will share in all that belongs to Christ.

HEBREWS 3:14 NLT

The LORD is trustworthy in all He promises and faithful in all He does.

PSALM 145:13 NIV

It is better to take refuge in the LORD than to trust in people.

PSALM 118:8 NLT

BE STRONG

— IN THE —

LORD

AND IN

HIS MIGHTY

POWER.

EPHESIANS 6:10

YOUR SOURCE OF STRENGTH

We all need spiritual strength – no matter how strong we are physically or mentally. Christ is the only one who can give you that strength. Accept Christ's offer of redemption and the strength that He promises you.

Acknowledge that God's strength is not your strength, and realize your dependence on Him. Feed your faith by remaining in God's presence and acknowledge the rulership of Christ. Go to the source of spiritual strength, Jesus Christ, and renew your strength every day.

In my weakness I come to You,
Lord Jesus, to draw from Your strength.

AMEN.

God is our refuge and strength, an ever-present help in trouble.

PSALM 46:1 NIV

I can do all things through Christ who strengthens me.

PHILIPPIANS 4:13 NKJV

God arms me with strength, and He makes my way perfect. He makes me as surefooted as a deer, enabling me to stand on mountain heights. He trains my hands for battle; He strengthens my arm to draw a bronze bow.

PSALM 18:32-34 NLT

The LORD gives strength to His people;
the LORD blesses His people with peace.

PSALM 29:11 NIV

"My grace is sufficient for you, for My strength is made perfect in weakness."

---

2 CORINTHIANS 12:9 NKJV

The Sovereign LORD is my strength; He makes my feet like the feet of a deer, He enables me to go on the heights.

HABAKKUK 3:19 NIV

"I will seek the lost, and I will bring back the strayed, and I will bind up the injured, and I will strengthen the weak."

EZEKIEL 34:16 ESV

The Lord is faithful, and He will strengthen and protect you from the evil one.

---

2 THESSALONIANS 3:3 NIV

"Do not fear, for I am with you; do not be dismayed, for I am your God. I will strengthen you and help you; I will uphold you with My righteous right hand."

ISAIAH 41:10 NIV

Honor and majesty are before Him; strength and gladness are in His place.

1 CHRONICLES 16:27 NKJV

My health may fail, and my spirit may grow weak, but God remains the strength of my heart; He is mine forever.

PSALM 73:26 NLT

"In repentance and rest is your salvation,
in quietness and trust is your strength."

ISAIAH 30:15 NIV

The LORD is my strength and my song; He has given me victory.

PSALM 118:14 NLT

May our Lord Jesus Christ Himself and God our Father, who loved us and by His grace gave us eternal encouragement and good hope, encourage your hearts and strengthen you in every good deed and word.

2 THESSALONIANS 2:16-17 NIV

In Your strength I can crush an army; with my God I can scale any wall.

PSALM 18:29 NLT

The LORD is my light and my salvation; whom shall I fear? The LORD is the strength of my life; of whom shall I be afraid?

PSALM 27:1 NKJV

Be on
YOUR GUARD;
STAND FIRM
— in the —
FAITH;
be courageous;
BE STRONG.
1 Corinthians 16:13

WHAT IS FAITH?

Faith is the weak hand I hold out to accept the salvation that Jesus made possible. God wants all people to be saved, but only faith in Jesus Christ can save us.

When you go on a train journey, the conductor will get to your compartment at some stage. He will not inquire about your family or your status in society. All he will say is, "Ticket please!" On our journey to eternity, the ticket we will be asked for is, "Do you have faith?" This really is an inevitable truth.

Holy Spirit of God, You who work faith in us, help me, in all circumstances, to cling firmly to my faith in God, through Jesus Christ alone.

AMEN.

We live by faith, not by sight.

---

2 CORINTHIANS 5:7 NIV

"I tell you the truth, if you have faith and don't doubt, you can do things like this and much more. You can even say to this mountain, 'May you be lifted up and thrown into the sea,' and it will happen."

MATTHEW 21:21 NLT

We fix our eyes not on what is seen, but on what is unseen, since what is seen is temporary, but what is unseen is eternal.

---

2 CORINTHIANS 4:18 NIV

"I tell you the truth, if you had faith even as small as a mustard seed, you could say to this mountain, 'Move from here to there,' and it would move. Nothing would be impossible."

MATTHEW 17:20 NLT

Be on your guard; stand firm in the faith;
be courageous; be strong.

---

1 CORINTHIANS 16:13 NIV

Now faith is the substance of things hoped for,
the evidence of things not seen.

HEBREWS 11:1 NKJV

In the gospel the righteousness of God is revealed –
a righteousness that is by faith from first to last,
just as it is written: "The righteous will live by faith."

ROMANS 1:17 NIV

Because of Christ and our faith in Him, we can now
come boldly and confidently into God's presence.

EPHESIANS 3:12 NLT

In all circumstances take up the shield of faith, with which you can extinguish all the flaming darts of the evil one.

EPHESIANS 6:16 ESV

Trust in the LORD with all your heart; do not depend on your own understanding. Seek His will in all you do, and He will show you which path to take.

PROVERBS 3:5-6 NLT

Make every effort to supplement your faith with virtue, and virtue with knowledge, and knowledge with self-control, and self-control with steadfastness, and steadfastness with godliness, and godliness with brotherly affection, and brotherly affection with love.

---

2 PETER 1:5-7 ESV

Faith comes from hearing the message, and the message is heard through the word about Christ.

ROMANS 10:17 NIV

Without faith it is impossible to please Him, for he who comes to God must believe that He is, and that He is a rewarder of those who diligently seek Him.

HEBREWS 11:6 NKJV

For I can do everything through Christ, who gives me strength.

PHILIPPIANS 4:13 NLT

Everyone who believes that Jesus is the Christ has been born of God, and everyone who loves the Father loves whoever has been born of Him.

1 JOHN 5:1 ESV

I have fought the good fight, I have finished the race, I have kept the faith.

2 TIMOTHY 4:7 NIV

HOPE
IN THE LORD!
— FOR WITH —
THE LORD
THERE IS
STEADFAST LOVE,
AND WITH
HIM IS
PLENTIFUL
REDEMPTION.
PSALM 130:7

HOPE IN THE LORD

The best way to deal with the challenges of life is to trust in the Lord and give Him full control of your life. Allow His Holy Spirit to influence you and to control every word and decision.

When you know that the Prince of Peace is your guide and teacher you will be able to cope with any situation. You will be victorious no matter what life has in store for you.

You are my keeper, O Lord my God. I place myself under Your control and in Your care. That is why I am assured of Your peace.

AMEN.

Those who hope in the LORD will renew their strength. They will soar on wings like eagles; they will run and not grow weary, they will walk and not be faint.

ISAIAH 40:31 NIV

Blessed are those whose hope is in the LORD their God.

PSALM 146:5 NIV

May the God of hope fill you with all joy and peace as you trust in Him, so that you may overflow with hope by the power of the Holy Spirit.

ROMANS 15:13 NIV

Having hope will give you courage. You will be protected and will rest in safety.

JOB 11:18 NLT

We have this hope as an anchor for the soul, firm and secure. It enters the inner sanctuary behind the curtain, where our forerunner, Jesus, has entered on our behalf.

HEBREWS 6:19-20 NIV

Hope will not lead to disappointment. For we know how dearly God loves us, because He has given us the Holy Spirit to fill our hearts with His love.

ROMANS 5:5 NLT

The eye of the LORD is on those who fear Him, on those who hope in His steadfast love.

PSALM 33:18 ESV

You answer us with awesome deeds of righteousness, O God our Savior, the hope of all the ends of the earth and of the farthest seas.

PSALM 65:5 NIV

My help comes from the LORD, who made heaven and earth!

PSALM 121:2 NLT

I pray that the eyes of your heart may be enlightened in order that you may know the hope to which He has called you.

EPHESIANS 1:18-19 NIV

I saw the Lord always before me … therefore my heart is glad and my tongue rejoices; my body also will rest in hope.

ACTS 2:25-26 NIV

The needy shall not always be forgotten, and the hope of the poor shall not perish forever.

PSALM 9:18 ESV

Hope deferred makes the heart sick, but a dream fulfilled is a tree of life.

PROVERBS 13:12 NLT

The LORD is good to those whose hope is in Him, to the one who seeks Him.

LAMENTATIONS 3:25 NIV

The LORD's delight is in those who fear Him, those who put their hope in His unfailing love.

PSALM 147:11 NLT

Be joyful in hope, patient in affliction, faithful in prayer.

ROMANS 12:12 NIV

Do not be
ANXIOUS
ABOUT ANYTHING,
— but in —
EVERYTHING
BY PRAYER
and
SUPPLICATION
WITH THANKSGIVING
let your requests
BE MADE KNOWN
to God.

Philippians 4:6

HOW TO GET RID OF

ANXIETY

It isn't hard work that causes mental, spiritual and ultimately physical breakdown – it's worry.

Having a practical faith in the omnipotence of God and His purpose for your life is essential. The conviction that all things work together for the good of those who love God should be the dominant thought in your mind. Then you will experience the renewing power of a living faith, which is the death-knell of all worry.

Merciful Lord, from today onwards I am determined not to allow worry to spoil the beauty of my life or to destroy my faith in You.

AMEN.

Cast all your anxiety on Him because He cares for you.

1 PETER 5:7 NIV

Commit everything you do to the LORD. Trust Him, and He will help you.

PSALM 37:5 NLT

"So do not fear, for I am with you; do not be dismayed, for I am your God."

ISAIAH 41:10 NIV

The LORD is my light and my salvation; whom shall I fear? The LORD is the strength of my life; of whom shall I be afraid?

PSALM 27:1 NKJV

Do not be anxious about anything, but in every situation, by prayer and petition, with thanksgiving, present your requests to God. And the peace of God, which transcends all understanding, will guard your hearts and your minds in Christ Jesus.

PHILIPPIANS 4:6-7 NIV

Even though I walk through the valley of the shadow of death, I will fear no evil, for You are with me; Your rod and Your staff, they comfort me.

PSALM 23:4 NIV

I have set the LORD always before me. Because He is at my right hand, I will not be shaken.

PSALM 16:8 NIV

"Do not be afraid and do not panic before them. For the LORD your God will personally go ahead of you. He will neither fail you nor abandon you."

DEUTERONOMY 31:6 NLT

"It is the Lord who goes before you. He will be with you; He will not leave you or forsake you. Do not fear or be dismayed."

DEUTERONOMY 31:8 ESV

"Therefore I tell you, do not be anxious about your life, what you will eat or what you will drink. Look at the birds of the air: they neither sow nor reap nor gather into barns, and yet your heavenly Father feeds them. Are you not of more value than they?"

MATTHEW 6:25-26 ESV

Be strong, and do not fear, for your God is coming to destroy your enemies. He is coming to save you.

ISAIAH 35:4 NLT

"Do not be anxious about how you should defend yourself or what you should say, for the Holy Spirit will teach you in that very hour what you ought to say."

LUKE 12:11-12 ESV

You will keep in perfect peace all who trust in You, all whose thoughts are fixed on You! Trust in the LORD always, for the LORD GOD is the eternal Rock.

ISAIAH 26:3-4 NLT

"Be still, and know that I am God."

PSALM 46:10 ESV

"Fear not, for I have redeemed you; I have called you by your name; you are Mine."

ISAIAH 43:1 NKJV

When I am afraid, I will put my trust in You.

PSALM 56:3 NLT

"Therefore do not be anxious about tomorrow, for tomorrow will be anxious for itself. Sufficient for the day is its own trouble."

MATTHEW 6:34 ESV

"BE STRONG
AND COURAGEOUS.
— DO NOT —
BE AFRAID;
— DO NOT —
BE DISCOURAGED,
FOR THE
LORD YOUR GOD
WILL BE
WITH YOU
WHEREVER
YOU GO."
JOSHUA 1:9

GOD IS WITH YOU

God is present in every situation in life. When you stand in awe before the beauty of a sunset or are astonished by the wonder of a sunrise; when bird-song fills you with excitement or the laughter of playing children gladdens your heart; when you look with reverence at the grandeur of the mountains or the splendor of the restless ocean; when you admire nature's wealth of flowers: be assured of God's presence! Look around: God is everywhere.

Omnipresent God, today I realize once again the wonder of Your love and I know that You are with me.

AMEN.

"Where two or three are gathered together in My name, I am there in the midst of them."

MATTHEW 18:20 NKJV

Let us hold fast the confession of our hope without wavering, for He who promised is faithful.

HEBREWS 10:23 ESV

Can you solve the mysteries of God? Can you discover everything about the Almighty? Such knowledge is higher than the heavens – and who are you? It is deeper than the underworld – what do you know? It is broader than the earth and wider than the sea.

JOB 11:7-9 NLT

"Anyone who loves Me will obey My teaching. My Father will love them, and We will come to them and make Our home with them.

JOHN 14:23 NIV

Because of Christ and our faith in Him, we can now come boldly and confidently into God's presence.

EPHESIANS 3:12 NLT

Surely Your goodness and unfailing love will pursue me all the days of my life, and I will live in the house of the LORD forever.

PSALM 23:6 NLT

The LORD your God is with you, the Mighty Warrior who saves. He will take great delight in you; in His love He will no longer rebuke you, but will rejoice over you with singing.

ZEPHANIAH 3:17 NIV

For the word of God is alive and active. Sharper than any double-edged sword, it penetrates even to dividing soul and spirit, joints and marrow; it judges the thoughts and attitudes of the heart. Nothing in all creation is hidden from God's sight. Everything is uncovered and laid bare before the eyes of Him to whom we must give account.

HEBREWS 4:12-13 NIV

"Can anyone hide from Me in a secret place? Am I not everywhere in all the heavens and earth?" says the LORD.

JEREMIAH 23:24 NLT

For this is what the high and exalted One says – He who lives forever, whose name is holy: "I live in a high and holy place, but also with the one who is contrite and lowly in spirit, to revive the spirit of the lowly and to revive the heart of the contrite."

ISAIAH 57:15 NIV

The eyes of the LORD are in every place, keeping watch on the evil and the good.

PROVERBS 15:3 NKJV

"I will be your God throughout your lifetime – until your hair is white with age. I made you, and I will care for you. I will carry you along and save you."

ISAIAH 46:4 NLT

He is before all things, and in Him all things hold together.

COLOSSIANS 1:17 ESV

"If you look for Me wholeheartedly, you will find Me."

JEREMIAH 29:13 NLT

"Where were you when I laid the foundations of the earth? Tell Me, if you have understanding. Who determined its measurements? Surely you know! Or who stretched the line upon it? To what were its foundations fastened? Or who laid its cornerstone, when the morning stars sang together, and all the sons of God shouted for joy?"

JOB 38:4-7 NKJV

God watches how people live; He sees everything they do.

JOB 34:21 NLT

God will
GENEROUSLY
provide all
YOU NEED.
— Then you —
WILL ALWAYS
have
EVERYTHING
YOU NEED
and plenty
left over
TO SHARE
with others.

2 Corinthians 9:8

GOD WILL

PROVIDE

God provides for your daily needs, however meager it may seem at times. He knows your needs and is prepared to provide for you through the wealth and abundance of Jesus Christ.

Your heavenly Father has assured you that He will never abandon you. He is constantly at your side, waiting for you to turn to Him for help, which He is always ready and willing to give.

Gracious Father God, thank You for providing me with everything I could ever need and more.

AMEN.

"Your Father knows what you need before you ask Him."

MATTHEW 6:8 NIV

He provides food for those who fear Him;
He remembers His covenant forever.

PSALM 111:5 ESV

God shall supply all your need according to His riches in glory by Christ Jesus.

PHILIPPIANS 4:19 NKJV

"Give, and it will be given to you. A good measure, pressed down, shaken together and running over, will be poured into your lap. For with the measure you use, it will be measured to you."

LUKE 6:38 NIV

"Therefore do not be anxious, saying, 'What shall we eat?' or 'What shall we drink?' or 'What shall we wear?' For the Gentiles seek after all these things, and your heavenly Father knows that you need them all."

MATTHEW 6:31-32 ESV

"Seek the Kingdom of God above all else, and live righteously, and He will give you everything you need."

MATTHEW 6:33 NLT

"Consider the ravens, for they neither sow nor reap, which have neither storehouse nor barn; and God feeds them. Of how much more value are you than the birds?"

LUKE 12:24 NKJV

"I will open the windows of heaven for you. I will pour out a blessing so great you won't have enough room to take it in. Try it! Put Me to the test!"

MALACHI 3:10 NLT

The lions may grow weak and hungry, but those who seek the LORD lack no good thing.

PSALM 34:10 NIV

The LORD is my shepherd; I have all that I need.

PSALM 23:1 NLT

He will give the rain for your land in its season, the early rain and the later rain, that you may gather in your grain and your wine and your oil. And He will give grass in your fields for your livestock, and you shall eat and be full.

DEUTERONOMY 11:14-15 ESV

"Every moving thing that lives shall be food for you. I have given you all things, even as the green herbs."

GENESIS 9:3 NKJV

You care for the land and water it; You enrich it abundantly. The streams of God are filled with water to provide the people with grain, for so You have ordained it.

PSAL[illegible] NIV

"Seek the Kingdom of God above all else, and [illegible] will give you everything you need."

LUKE 12:31 NLT

Fear the LORD, you His godly people, for those who fear Him will have all they need.

PSALM 34:9 NLT

He who supplies seed to the sower and bread for food will also supply and increase your store of seed and will enlarge the harvest of your righteousness.

---

2 CORINTHIANS 9:10 NIV

THE LORD

WILL GUIDE

YOU ALWAYS;

HE WILL

SATISFY

YOUR NEEDS

IN A

SUNSCORCHED LAND

AND WILL

STRENGTHEN

YOUR FRAME.

Isaiah 58:11

GOD WILL

LEAD YOU

To this day, God leads us just as He led the people of Israel: through deep waters to the pristine shores of eternity. He will grab you with His rescuing right hand. He will strengthen you. He will help you.

God alone can lead you in His path of righteousness, and as He leads you, He will grant you the ability to handle every situation so that you may have the peace of mind that banishes all fear and anxiety.

Thank You, Good Shepherd, that I am in Your caring hand at all times.

AMEN.

Show me Your ways, LORD, teach me Your paths. Guide me in Your truth and teach me, for You are God my Savior, and my hope is in You all day long.

PSALM 25:4-5 NIV

Send out Your light and Your truth; let them guide me. Let them lead me to Your holy mountain, to the place where You live.

PSALM 43:3 NLT

"Call to Me, and I will answer you, and show you great and mighty things, which you do not know."

JEREMIAH 33:3 NKJV

Your word is a lamp to guide my feet and a light for my path.

PSALM 119:105 NLT

Teach me to do Your will, for You are my God!
Let Your good Spirit lead me on level ground!

PSALM 143:10 ESV

May the Lord direct your hearts into God's love and Christ's perseverance.

---

2 THESSALONIANS 3:5 NIV

The LORD directs the steps of the godly. He delights in every detail of their lives. Though they stumble, they will never fall, for the LORD holds them by the hand.

PSALM 37:23-24 NLT

Whether you turn to the right or to the left, your ears will hear a voice behind you, saying, "This is the way; walk in it."

ISAIAH 30:21 NIV

Direct my steps by Your word, and let no iniquity have dominion over me.

PSALM 119:133 NKJV

All who are led by the Spirit of God are children of God.

ROMANS 8:14 NLT

"I will go before you and make the crooked places straight; I will break in pieces the gates of bronze and cut the bars of iron."

ISAIAH 45:2 NKJV

He guides the humble in what is right and teaches them His way.

PSALM 25:9 NIV

The LORD is good and does what is right; He shows the proper path to those who go astray.

PSALM 25:8 NLT

God is our God for ever and ever; He will be our guide even to the end.

PSALM 48:14 NIV

The LORD says, "I will guide you along the best pathway for your life. I will advise you and watch over you."

PSALM 32:8 NLT

May He give you the desire of your heart and make all your plans succeed.

PSALM 20:4 NIV

Whoever
DWELLS
in the
SHELTER
of the
Most High
WILL REST
in the
SHADOW
of the
Almighty.

Psalm 91:1

REST IN GOD'S LOVE

Throughout your life, it is necessary to find a measure of stability in order to handle each day's challenges. To achieve this, just look around you and take note of the incredible wonder of God's creation.

Absorb the beauty of nature, music and art. But, above all, remember that God has revealed His love for you through the sacrifice of His Son on the cross. Hold unflinchingly to this truth and find rest in God's love.

Jesus, Source of true love, let us rest in Your love.

AMEN.

The LORD replied, "My Presence will go with you, and I will give you rest."

EXODUS 33:14 NIV

Jesus said, "Come to Me, all of you who are weary and carry heavy burdens, and I will give you rest. Take My yoke upon you. Let Me teach you, because I am humble and gentle at heart, and you will find rest for your souls. For My yoke is easy to bear, and the burden I give you is light."

MATTHEW 11:28-30 NLT

He said to them, "Come away by yourselves to a desolate place and rest a while."

MARK 6:31 ESV

Rest in the LORD, and wait patiently for Him; do not fret because of him who prospers in his way, because of the man who brings wicked schemes to pass.

PSALM 37:7 NKJV

This is what the Sovereign Lord, the Holy One of Israel, says: "Only in returning to Me and resting in Me will you be saved. In quietness and confidence is your strength."

ISAIAH 30:15 NLT

In peace I will lie down and sleep, for You alone, O Lord, will keep me safe.

PSALM 4:8 NLT

The fear of the Lord leads to life; then one rests content, untouched by trouble.

PROVERBS 19:23 NIV

"Peace I leave with you; My peace I give you. I do not give to you as the world gives. Do not let your hearts be troubled and do not be afraid."

JOHN 14:27 NIV

"I have told you all this so that you may have peace in Me. Here on earth you will have many trials and sorrows. But take heart, because I have overcome the world."

JOHN 16:33 NLT

Truly my soul finds rest in God; my salvation comes from Him.

PSALM 62:1 NIV

The work of righteousness will be peace, and the effect of righteousness, quietness and assurance forever.

ISAIAH 32:17 NKJV

The LORD gives strength to His people;
the LORD blesses His people with peace.

PSALM 29:11 NIV

Great peace have those who love Your law,
and nothing can make them stumble.

PSALM 119:165 NIV

Let the peace of Christ rule in your hearts.

COLOSSIANS 3:15 ESV

You will keep in perfect peace those whose minds are steadfast, because they trust in You.

ISAIAH 26:3 NIV

God is not a God of confusion but of peace.

1 CORINTHIANS 14:33 ESV

The God of peace be with you all.

ROMANS 15:33 NIV

THE LORD
GIVES WISDOM;
FROM
HIS MOUTH
COME
KNOWLEDGE
AND
UNDERSTANDING.

PROVERBS 2:6

WISDOM
COMES FROM GOD

A spiritual person has discovered the true Source of wisdom. He has peace and inner strength that comes from fellowship with the Holy Spirit, and lives his life with contentment and purpose.

Therefore, spend time with God, allowing the fragrance of His life to permeate your life so that you can serve Him in truth, and so that His wisdom, peace, and strength can flow through you.

God of wisdom, make me wise in Your ways, through the Spirit. Let me wait for You constantly so that I can develop an intimate relationship with You.

AMEN.

The law of the LORD is perfect, refreshing the soul. The statutes of the LORD are trustworthy, making wise the simple.

PSALM 19:7 NIV

If you need wisdom, ask our generous God, and He will give it to you. He will not rebuke you for asking.

JAMES 1:5 NLT

"I will instruct you and teach you in the way you should go; I will counsel you with My loving eye on you."

PSALM 32:8 NIV

The entrance of Your words gives light; it gives understanding to the simple.

PSALM 119:130 NKJV

God gives wisdom, knowledge, and joy to those who please Him.

ECCLESIASTES 2:26 NLT

To God belong wisdom and power; counsel and understanding are His.

JOB 12:13 NIV

Praise the name of God forever and ever, for He has all wisdom and power. He gives wisdom to the wise and knowledge to the scholars.

DANIEL 2:20-21 NLT

For the LORD gives wisdom; from His mouth come knowledge and understanding.

PROVERBS 2:6 NIV

Do not forsake wisdom, and she will protect you; love her, and she will watch over you.

PROVERBS 4:6 NIV

Fear of the LORD is the foundation of true wisdom. All who obey His commandments will grow in wisdom.

PSALM 111:10 NLT

The wisdom that comes from heaven is first of all pure; then peace-loving, considerate, submissive, full of mercy and good fruit, impartial and sincere.

JAMES 3:17 NIV

Wisdom is sweet to your soul. If you find it, you will have a bright future, and your hopes will not be cut short.

PROVERBS 24:14 NLT

By wisdom a house is built, and by understanding it is established; by knowledge the rooms are filled with all precious and pleasant riches.

PROVERBS 24:3-4 ESV

Wisdom will multiply your days and add years to your life.

PROVERBS 9:11 NLT

The fear of the LORD is the beginning of wisdom, and knowledge of the Holy One is understanding.

PROVERBS 9:10 NIV

Wisdom will enter your heart, and knowledge will fill you with joy. Wise choices will watch over you. Understanding will keep you safe. Wisdom will save you from evil people, from those whose words are twisted.

PROVERBS 2:10-12 NLT

GIVE THANKS
TO THE LORD,
FOR HE IS GOOD!
HIS FAITHFUL
LOVE
ENDURES FOREVER.
1 CHRONICLES 16:34

A SPIRIT OF

THANKSGIVING

Thanksgiving is a powerful force in your spiritual life. It can dispel the dark clouds of depression and despair. The only way to release the power of thanksgiving is to practice it every day.

Start each day with a sincere prayer of appreciation to your heavenly Father for the gift of life. You will discover that by doing this, you will establish an atmosphere for the day that will cause you to live in victory.

Holy Lord Jesus, I praise You because of Your great love for me. Thank You for the gift of life – abundant and eternal life that You give to me.

AMEN.

Give thanks to the LORD and proclaim His greatness. Let the whole world know what He has done.

PSALM 105:1 NLT

Thanks be to God, who in Christ always leads us in triumphal procession, and through us spreads the fragrance of the knowledge of Him everywhere.

---

2 CORINTHIANS 2:14 ESV

It is good to give thanks to the LORD, to sing praises to the Most High. It is good to proclaim Your unfailing love in the morning, Your faithfulness in the evening.

PSALM 92:1-2 NLT

Come, let us sing for joy to the LORD; let us shout aloud to the Rock of our salvation. Let us come before Him with thanksgiving and extol Him with music and song. For the LORD is the great God, the great King above all gods.

PSALM 95:1-3 NIV

You made all the delicate, inner parts of my body and knit me together in my mother's womb. Thank You for making me so wonderfully complex! Your workmanship is marvelous – how well I know it.

PSALM 139:13-14 NLT

Thanks be to God for His indescribable gift!

---

2 CORINTHIANS 9:15 NKJV

Enter His gates with thanksgiving and His courts with praise; give thanks to Him and praise His name.

PSALM 100:4 NIV

Thank God! He gives us victory over sin and death through our Lord Jesus Christ.

---

1 CORINTHIANS 15:57 NLT

Oh give thanks to the LORD; call upon His name; make known His deeds among the peoples!

---

1 CHRONICLES 16:8 ESV

We give thanks to You, O God, we give thanks! For Your wondrous works declare that Your name is near.

PSALM 75:1 NKJV

May you be filled with joy, always thanking the Father.

COLOSSIANS 1:11-12 NLT

Sing to the LORD with thanksgiving; sing praises on the harp to our God, who covers the heavens with clouds, who prepares rain for the earth, who makes grass to grow on the mountains.

PSALM 147:7-8 NKJV

I will give thanks to the LORD with my whole heart; I will recount all of Your wonderful deeds. I will be glad and exult in You; I will sing praise to Your name, O Most High.

PSALM 9:1-2 ESV

Sing and make music from your heart to the Lord, always giving thanks to God the Father for everything, in the name of our Lord Jesus Christ.

EPHESIANS 5:19-20 NIV

Whatever you do, in word or deed, do everything in the name of the Lord Jesus, giving thanks to God the Father through Him.

COLOSSIANS 3:17 ESV

Be thankful in all circumstances, for this is God's will for you who belong to Christ Jesus.

---

1 THESSALONIANS 5:18 NLT

THE PRAYER

OF A

RIGHTEOUS PERSON

IS POWERFUL

AND EFFECTIVE.

JAMES 5:16

POWERFUL

QUIET TIME

True prayer is to personally experience the presence of the living Christ in your quiet times and right through the day. It is the joyous assurance that the Lord keeps His promise and that He lives in you and you in Him (see Jn. 15:4).

Such prayer becomes a faith exercise that teaches you that, as you lay your requests before Him, He will give you what you need according to His wisdom, and you will recognize and accept His answers. Gratefully accept His will and then experience His perfect peace in your heart.

Lord my God, it is with gratitude and humility that I accept Your will for my life, for in You is perfect wisdom.

AMEN.

Devote yourselves to prayer with an alert mind and a thankful heart.

COLOSSIANS 4:2 NLT

Pray in the Spirit on all occasions with all kinds of prayers and requests. With this in mind, be alert and always keep on praying for all the Lord's people.

EPHESIANS 6:18 NIV

Let my prayer be set before You as incense, the lifting up of my hands as the evening sacrifice.

PSALM 141:2 NKJV

"When you pray, go into your room, close the door and pray to your Father, who is unseen. Then your Father, who sees what is done in secret, will reward you."

MATTHEW 6:6 NIV

The LORD delights in the prayers of the upright.

PROVERBS 15:8 NLT

Rejoice always, pray continually, give thanks in all circumstances; for this is God's will for you in Christ Jesus.

---

1 THESSALONIANS 5:16-18 NIV

"When you pray, do not use vain repetitions as the heathen do. For they think that they will be heard for their many words. Therefore do not be like them. For your Father knows the things you have need of before you ask Him."

MATTHEW 6:7-8 NKJV

"Watch and pray so that you will not fall into temptation. The spirit is willing, but the flesh is weak."

MATTHEW 26:41 NIV

Give ear, O Lord, to my prayer; listen to my plea for grace.

PSALM 86:6 ESV

Is anyone among you in trouble? Let them pray. Is anyone happy? Let them sing songs of praise. Is anyone among you sick? Let them call the elders of the church to pray over them and anoint them with oil in the name of the Lord.

JAMES 5:13-14 NIV

I confessed all my sins to You and stopped trying to hide my guilt. I said to myself, "I will confess my rebellion to the Lord." And You forgave me! All my guilt is gone. Therefore, let all the godly pray to You while there is still time, that they may not drown in the floodwaters of judgment.

PSALM 32:5-6 NLT

"If you believe, you will receive whatever you ask for in prayer."

MATTHEW 21:22 NIV

This is the confidence that we have in Him, that if we ask anything according to His will, He hears us. And if we know that He hears us, whatever we ask, we know that we have the petitions that we have asked of Him.

---

1 JOHN 5:14-15 NKJV

The eyes of the Lord are on the righteous and His ears are attentive to their prayer.

---

1 PETER 3:12 NIV

"I tell you, you can pray for anything, and if you believe that you've received it, it will be yours."

MARK 11:24 NLT

Truly God has listened; He has attended to the voice of my prayer. Blessed be God, because He has not rejected my prayer or removed His steadfast love from me!

PSALM 66:19-20 ESV

DRAW NEAR

TO GOD,

AND

HE WILL

DRAW NEAR

TO YOU.

JAMES 4:8

SEEKING GOD

To seek God is an extremely important and wonderful task. If you focus your entire being on seeking Him, you can rest assured that your "seeking" will end in "finding".

God is available to everyone who seeks Him in earnest. He is not in hiding, or a secret God. He comes looking for you in His Son's crib and at the Cross of Golgotha.

Loving Father, thank You that You found me and that You wrapped me in Your grace.

AMEN.

Those who know Your name will put their trust in You; for You, LORD, have not forsaken those who seek You.

PSALM 9:10 NKJV

My heart says of You, "Seek His face!" Your face, LORD, I will seek. Do not hide Your face from me, do not turn Your servant away in anger; You have been my helper.

PSALM 27:8-9 NIV

Seek the LORD your God, and you will find Him if you seek Him with all your heart and with all your soul.

DEUTERONOMY 4:29 NKJV

"Ask, and it will be given to you; seek, and you will find; knock, and it will be opened to you. For everyone who asks receives, and the one who seeks finds, and to the one who knocks it will be opened."

MATTHEW 7:7-8 ESV

I love those who love me, and those who seek me diligently will find me.

PROVERBS 8:17 NKJV

"Whoever believes in Me, as Scripture has said, rivers of living water will flow from within them." By this He meant the Spirit, whom those who believed in Him were later to receive.

JOHN 7:38-39 NIV

Seek the LORD and His strength; seek His face evermore!

PSALM 105:4 NKJV

The LORD looks down from heaven on all mankind to see if there are any who understand, any who seek God.

PSALM 14:2 NIV

The LORD is with you while you are with Him. If you seek Him, He will be found by you, but if you forsake Him, He will forsake you.

---

2 CHRONICLES 15:2 ESV

The lions may grow weak and hungry, but those who seek the LORD lack no good thing.

PSALM 34:10 NIV

He made from one man every nation of mankind to live on all the face of the earth, having determined allotted periods and the boundaries of their dwelling place, that they should seek God, and perhaps feel their way toward Him and find Him. Yet He is actually not far from each one of us.

ACTS 17:26-27 ESV

If then you were raised with Christ, seek those things which are above, where Christ is, sitting at the right hand of God. Set your mind on things above, not on things on the earth.

COLOSSIANS 3:1-2 NKJV

You, God, are my God, earnestly I seek You.

PSALM 63:1 NIV

"Seek the Kingdom of God above all else, and live righteously, and He will give you everything you need."

MATTHEW 6:33 NLT

Seek the LORD while He may be found; call upon Him while He is near.

ISAIAH 55:6 ESV

The LORD sees every heart and knows every plan and thought. If you seek Him, you will find Him. But if you forsake Him, He will reject you forever.

---

1 CHRONICLES 28:9 NLT

Devote your heart and soul to seeking the LORD your God.

---

1 CHRONICLES 22:19 NIV

BLESSED
IS THE
ONE WHO
PERSEVERES
UNDER TRIAL
— BECAUSE, —
HAVING STOOD
THE TEST,
THAT PERSON
WILL RECEIVE
THE CROWN
OF LIFE
— THAT THE —
LORD HAS
PROMISED
TO THOSE
WHO LOVE HIM.

JAMES 1:12

PERSEVERANCE IS KEY

Patient endurance is one of the basic qualities of the Christian believer. It is making a comeback after every setback and starting over after each failure; it is keeping your eyes on the horizon.

If you have stumbled in your faith somewhere along the way, don't lose heart. Don't expect an easy and prosperous journey. Expect hardship and disappointment, but hold on to Jesus – until the very end.

God of grace, grant me the patience to endure and persevere to the very end.

AMEN.

I press on toward the goal to win the prize for which God has called me heavenward in Christ Jesus.

PHILIPPIANS 3:14 NIV

Everything that was written in the past was written to teach us, so that through the endurance taught in the Scriptures and the encouragement they provide we might have hope.

ROMANS 15:4 NIV

Take up your positions; stand firm and see the deliverance the LORD will give you.

---

2 CHRONICLES 20:17 NIV

We have come to share in Christ, if indeed we hold our original conviction firmly to the very end.

HEBREWS 3:14 NIV

Let us not become weary in doing good, for at the proper time we will reap a harvest if we do not give up.

GALATIANS 6:9 NIV

You need to persevere so that when you have done the will of God, you will receive what He has promised.

HEBREWS 10:36 NIV

Always give yourselves fully to the work of the Lord, because you know that your labor in the Lord is not in vain.

1 CORINTHIANS 15:58 NIV

Make every effort to confirm your calling and election. For if you do these things, you will never stumble, and you will receive a rich welcome into the eternal kingdom of our Lord and Savior Jesus Christ.

2 PETER 1:10-11 NIV

Consider it pure joy, my brothers and sisters, whenever you face trials of many kinds, because you know that the testing of your faith develops perseverance. Let perseverance finish its work so that you may be mature and complete, not lacking anything.

JAMES 1:2-4 NIV

We also glory in our sufferings, because we know that suffering produces perseverance; perseverance, character; and character, hope. And hope does not disappoint us, because God's love has been poured out into our hearts through the Holy Spirit, who has been given us.

ROMANS 5:3-5 NIV

Let us run with endurance the race God has set before us. We do this by keeping our eyes on Jesus, the champion who initiates and perfects our faith. Because of the joy awaiting Him, He endured the cross, disregarding its shame. Now He is seated in the place of honor beside God's throne.

HEBREWS 12:1-2 NLT

"He who endures to the end shall be saved."

MATTHEW 24:13 NKJV

May the God who gives endurance and encouragement give you a spirit of unity among yourselves as you follow Christ Jesus.

ROMANS 15:5 NIV

You need to persevere so that when you have done the will of God, you will receive what He has promised.

HEBREWS 10:36 NIV

Make every effort to add to your faith goodness; and to goodness, knowledge; and to knowledge, self-control; and to self-control, perseverance; and to perseverance, godliness; and to godliness, mutual affection; and to mutual affection, love. For if you possess these qualities in increasing measure, they will keep you from being ineffective and unproductive in your knowledge of our Lord Jesus Christ.

---

2 PETER 1:5-8 NIV

Be strong and do not give up, for your work will be rewarded.

---

2 CHRONICLES 15:7 NIV

WHETHER YOU EAT
OR DRINK,
OR WHATEVER
YOU DO,
DO IT ALL
FOR THE GLORY
OF GOD.

1 Corinthians 10:31

WORKING
FOR GOD'S GLORY

God expects Christians to perform their daily tasks with dedication and integrity, and to glorify Him in all things. However, He also expects you to spend time resting.

Remain sensitive to the voice of the Holy Spirit, then you will be able to give work and rest their rightful place in your daily routine, knowing that God will abundantly supply all your needs as you structure your life according to His will.

Please make me reliable in my daily tasks,
O Lord, as I do everything to Your glory.

AMEN.

The LORD your God will bless you in all your harvest and in all the work of your hands, and your joy will be complete.

DEUTERONOMY 16:15 NIV

"Be strong, all you people of the land," says the LORD, "and work; for I am with you," says the LORD of hosts.

HAGGAI 2:4 NKJV

You shall eat the fruit of the labor of your hands; you shall be blessed, and it shall be well with you.

PSALM 128:2 ESV

Whatever you do, in word or deed, do everything in the name of the Lord Jesus, giving thanks to God the Father through Him.

COLOSSIANS 3:17 NIV

God is not unjust. He will not forget how hard you have worked for Him and how you have shown your love to Him by caring for other believers, as you still do.

HEBREWS 6:10 NLT

My dear brothers and sisters, be strong and immovable. Always work enthusiastically for the Lord, for you know that nothing you do for the Lord is ever useless.

1 CORINTHIANS 15:58 NLT

Let the favor of the Lord our God be upon us,
and establish the work of our hands upon us;
yes, establish the work of our hands!

PSALM 90:17 ESV

Work brings profit, but mere talk leads to poverty! Wealth is a crown for the wise; the effort of fools yields only foolishness.

PROVERBS 14:23-24 NLT

Lazy people want much but get little, but those who work hard will prosper.

PROVERBS 13:4 NLT

Work hard and become a leader; be lazy and become a slave.

PROVERBS 12:24 NLT

A hard worker has plenty of food, but a person who chases fantasies has no sense.

PROVERBS 12:11 NLT

"Do not labor for the food which perishes, but for the food which endures to everlasting life, which the Son of Man will give you, because God the Father has set His seal on Him."

JOHN 6:27 NKJV

There is nothing better than to enjoy food and drink and to find satisfaction in work … these pleasures are from the hand of God.

ECCLESIASTES 2:24 NLT

From the fruit of their lips people are filled with good things, and the work of their hands brings them reward.

PROVERBS 12:14 NIV

There is nothing better for a person than to enjoy their work, because that is their lot.

ECCLESIASTES 3:22 NIV

I can do all things through Christ who strengthens me.

PHILIPPIANS 4:13 NKJV

THE PLANS
OF THE
LORD
STAND FIRM
FOREVER,
THE PURPOSES OF
HIS HEART
THROUGH ALL
GENERATIONS.

PSALM 33:11

A LIFE OF PURPOSE

As a dedicated Christian your highest goal should be to please God – and not yourself. This is the key to a purposeful and satisfying life.

There is no greater goal in life than to do the will of God. That is why you were born, and deviating from it leads only to frustration and dissatisfaction. Living to carry out God's will requires a high level of commitment. But it brings joy untold because it brings you in touch with the Source of joy and fills your life with riches and blessings that are the inheritance of those who love and serve Christ.

Lord, I commit myself to You anew, so that I can experience the joy of a purposeful life.

AMEN.

"Before I formed you in the womb I knew you,
and before you were born I consecrated you;
I appointed you a prophet to the nations."

JEREMIAH 1:5 ESV

You made all the delicate, inner parts of my body and knit me together in my mother's womb. Thank You for making me so wonderfully complex! Your workmanship is marvelous – how well I know it.

PSALM 139:13-14 NLT

For we are God's masterpiece. He has created us anew in Christ Jesus, so we can do the good things He planned for us long ago.

EPHESIANS 2:10 NLT

God created mankind in His own image, in the image of God He created them; male and female He created them.

GENESIS 1:27 NIV

"Everyone who is called by My name, whom I have created for My glory; I have formed him, yes, I have made him."

ISAIAH 43:7 NKJV

And the LORD God formed man of the dust of the ground, and breathed into his nostrils the breath of life; and man became a living being.

GENESIS 2:7 NKJV

Know that the LORD, He is God! It is He who made us, and we are His; we are His people, and the sheep of His pasture.

PSALM 100:3 ESV

Even before He made the world, God loved us and chose us in Christ to be holy and without fault in His eyes. God decided in advance to adopt us into His own family by bringing us to Himself through Jesus Christ.

EPHESIANS 1:4-5 NLT

The Spirit of God has made me; the breath of the Almighty gives me life.

JOB 33:4 NIV

"Are not two sparrows sold for a copper coin? And not one of them falls to the ground apart from your Father's will. But the very hairs of your head are all numbered. Do not fear therefore; you are of more value than many sparrows."

MATTHEW 10:29-31 NKJV

In Him also we have obtained an inheritance, being predestined according to the purpose of Him who works all things according to the counsel of His will, that we who first trusted in Christ should be to the praise of His glory.

EPHESIANS 1:11-12 NKJV

I run with purpose in every step. I am not just shadowboxing.

---

1 CORINTHIANS 9:26 NLT

What is man that You are mindful of him, and the son of man that You care for him? Yet You have made him a little lower than the heavenly beings and crowned him with glory and honor.

PSALM 8:4-5 ESV

Many are the plans in a person's heart, but it is the LORD's purpose that prevails.

PROVERBS 19:21 NIV

All the days ordained for me were written in Your book before one of them came to be.

PSALM 139:16 NIV

"You didn't choose Me. I chose you. I appointed you to go and produce lasting fruit, so that the Father will give you whatever you ask for, using My name."

JOHN 15:16 NLT

You are a
CHOSEN GENERATION,
A ROYAL PRIESTHOOD,
A HOLY NATION,
HIS OWN
SPECIAL PEOPLE,
— THAT YOU —
MAY PROCLAIM
THE PRAISES
OF HIM
WHO CALLED YOU
OUT OF DARKNESS
— INTO HIS —
MARVELOUS LIGHT.
1 Peter 2:9

CHOSEN TO SERVE

God called us to serve Him with joy, no matter how hard the task. Our life should radiate joy, because God gave us the privilege of being His children and working for Him.

We were chosen to serve in love. Without love, we cannot be ambassadors of the Source of all true love. It gives us a passion for souls and keeps us from competing with one another for petty honors. We are fellow-workers with Christ and our service and the fruit we bear should be evidence of all that is best and most noble in our lives.

I want to stay close to You, beloved Guide. I want to trust You always and remain faithful to You so that I can bear fruit for You in this world.

AMEN.

For He chose us in Him before the creation of the world to be holy and blameless in His sight. In love He predestined us for adoption to sonship through Jesus Christ, in accordance with His pleasure and will.

EPHESIANS 1:4-5 NIV

We are His workmanship, created in Christ Jesus for good works, which God prepared beforehand that we should walk in them.

EPHESIANS 2:10 NKJV

In Him we were also chosen, having been predestined according to the plan of Him who works out everything in conformity with the purpose of His will, in order that we, who were the first to put our hope in Christ, might be for the praise of His glory.

EPHESIANS 1:11-12 NIV

You have been set apart as holy to the LORD your God, and He has chosen you from all the nations of the earth to be His own special treasure.

DEUTERONOMY 14:2 NLT

God knew His people in advance, and He chose them to become like His Son, so that His Son would be the firstborn among many brothers and sisters. And having chosen them, He called them to come to Him. And having called them, He gave them right standing with Himself. And having given them right standing, He gave them His glory.

ROMANS 8:29-30 NLT

"You did not choose Me, but I chose you and appointed you that you should go and bear fruit and that your fruit should abide, so that whatever you ask the Father in My name, He may give it to you."

JOHN 15:16 ESV

You are a holy people to the LORD your God; the LORD your God has chosen you to be a people for Himself, a special treasure above all the peoples on the face of the earth.

DEUTERONOMY 7:6 NKJV

"Before I formed you in the womb I knew you, before you were born I set you apart; I appointed you as a prophet to the nations."

JEREMIAH 1:5 NIV

He is Lord of lords and King of kings; and those who are with Him are called, chosen, and faithful.

REVELATION 17:14 NKJV

To all who did receive Him, who believed in His name, He gave the right to become children of God, who were born, not of blood nor of the will of the flesh nor of the will of man, but of God.

JOHN 1:12-13 ESV

Know that the LORD has set apart for Himself him who is godly; the LORD will hear when I call to Him.

PSALM 4:3 NKJV

Once you were not a people, but now you are God's people; once you had not received mercy, but now you have received mercy.

1 PETER 2:10 ESV

He called you to salvation when we told you the Good News; now you can share in the glory of our Lord Jesus Christ.

2 THESSALONIANS 2:14 NLT

THE JOY

OF THE

LORD IS

YOUR STRENGTH.

NEHEMIAH 8:10

THERE IS JOY WITH GOD

Your Father takes joy in your life. He is happy when you are happy; He consoles you in sadness and grief; He supports you when the burden becomes too much for you; He helps you up when you stumble over obstacles and He enjoys your successes as you enjoy them yourself.

Through your communion with the living Christ, you live in the blessing of His presence every day. The more you praise and thank Him, the more happiness you glean from your spiritual life.

Savior, thank You for rejoicing in me as Your child. Fill me with Your peace and joy today.

AMEN.

This is the day that the LORD has made; let us rejoice and be glad in it.

PSALM 118:24 ESV

Those who sow with tears will reap with songs of joy.

PSALM 126:5 NIV

The LORD is my strength and song, and He has become my salvation.

PSALM 118:14 NKJV

Glory in His holy name; let the hearts of those who seek the LORD rejoice.

PSALM 105:3 NIV

"Rejoice because your names are written in heaven."

LUKE 10:20 NKJV

"Be happy! Yes, leap for joy! For a great reward awaits you in heaven."

LUKE 6:23 NLT

In Him our hearts rejoice, for we trust in His holy name.

PSALM 33:21 NIV

When Your words came, I ate them; they were my joy and my heart's delight.

JEREMIAH 15:16 NIV

You turned my wailing into dancing; You removed my sackcloth and clothed me with joy.

PSALM 30:11 NIV

The joy of the LORD is your strength.

NEHEMIAH 8:10 NKJV

Those who look to Him for help will be radiant with joy; no shadow of shame will darken their faces.

PSALM 34:5 NLT

Because You are my help, I sing in the shadow of Your wings.

PSALM 63:7 NIV

You have given me greater joy than those who have abundant harvests of grain and new wine.

PSALM 4:7 NLT

The precepts of the LORD are right, giving joy to the heart. The commands of the LORD are radiant, giving light to the eyes.

PSALM 19:8 NIV

Honor and majesty are before Him; strength and gladness are in His place.

---

1 CHRONICLES 16:27 NKJV

Let all those who seek You rejoice and be glad in You; and let those who love Your salvation say continually, "Let God be magnified!"

PSALM 70:4 NKJV

For His anger lasts only a moment, but His favor lasts a lifetime; weeping may stay for the night, but rejoicing comes in the morning.

PSALM 30:5 NIV

Light shines on the godly, and joy on those whose hearts are right.

PSALM 97:11 NLT

The LORD has done great things for us, and we are filled with joy.

PSALM 126:3 NIV

Shouts of joy and victory resound in the tents of the righteous: "The LORD's right hand has done mighty things!"

PSALM 118:15 NIV

BETTER

TO BE

PATIENT

THAN POWERFUL;

BETTER

TO HAVE

SELF-CONTROL

THAN TO

CONQUER A CITY.

PROVERBS 16:32

LEARNING TO BE

PATIENT

On many occasions we are required to provide some advice, support or companionship, and so often we respond only by showing our impatience.

Despite your busy life, Christ will always give you the time to do His work. Trust Him unconditionally and you too will be able to treat people with the same patience, compassion and empathy that He did. In this way you will become a source of encouragement, calmness and peace for others.

Lord Jesus, I open myself to Your Spirit of peace, patience and encouragement in my interaction with other people.

AMEN.

Be joyful in hope, patient in affliction, faithful in prayer.

ROMANS 12:12 NIV

I waited patiently for the LORD; He turned to me and heard my cry.

PSALM 40:1 NIV

Wait for the LORD; be strong and take heart and wait for the LORD.

PSALM 27:14 NIV

The end of a matter is better than its beginning, and patience is better than pride.

ECCLESIASTES 7:8 NIV

Through patience a ruler can be persuaded, and a gentle tongue can break a bone.

PROVERBS 25:15 NIV

If we look forward to something we don't yet have, we must wait patiently and confidently.

ROMANS 8:25 NLT

You need to persevere so that when you have done the will of God, you will receive what He has promised.

HEBREWS 10:36 NIV

As the elect of God, holy and beloved, put on tender mercies, kindness, humility, meekness, longsuffering.

COLOSSIANS 3:12 NKJV

Hope that is seen is no hope at all. Who hopes for what they already have?

ROMANS 8:24 NIV

Be completely humble and gentle; be patient, bearing with one another in love. Make every effort to keep the unity of the Spirit through the bond of peace.

EPHESIANS 4:2-3 NIV

Those who wait on the LORD shall renew their strength; they shall mount up with wings like eagles, they shall run and not be weary, they shall walk and not faint.

ISAIAH 40:31 NKJV

Rejoice in our confident hope. Be patient in trouble, and keep on praying.

ROMANS 12:12 NLT

The Lord is not slow in keeping His promise, as some understand slowness. Instead He is patient with you, not wanting anyone to perish, but everyone to come to repentance.

---

2 PETER 3:9 NIV

Be still before the LORD and wait patiently for Him;
do not fret when people succeed in their ways,
when they carry out their wicked schemes.
Refrain from anger and turn from wrath.

PSALM 37:7-8 NIV

It is good that one should wait quietly for the salvation of the LORD.

LAMENTATIONS 3:26 ESV

Hope that is seen is no hope at all. Who hopes for what they already have? But if we hope for what we do not yet have, we wait for it patiently.

ROMANS 8:24-25 NIV

You, Lord, are a compassionate and gracious God, slow to anger, abounding in love and faithfulness.

PSALM 86:15 NIV

All of you,
CLOTHE YOURSELVES
with
HUMILITY
TOWARD ONE
ANOTHER,
because,
"GOD OPPOSES
THE PROUD
BUT SHOWS
FAVOR TO
THE HUMBLE."

1 Peter 5:5

ACHIEVING HUMILITY

In the demanding world in which we live there are many people, especially in the business world, who look upon humility as a sign of weakness. However, the greatest Leader ever known to mankind is Jesus. His entire being reflected humility. People paid attention to what He said and did. They obeyed and followed Him. Even His enemies respected and admired Him.

To achieve success in life, temper everything you do with the spirit of the Master. Then you will undoubtedly gain the respect of others.

Lord Jesus, help me to follow Your example of humility. Protect me from the monster of pride.

AMEN.

Humble yourselves in the sight of the Lord, and He will lift you up.

JAMES 4:10 NKJV

True humility and fear of the LORD lead to riches, honor, and long life.

PROVERBS 22:4 NLT

"I will bless those who have humble and contrite hearts, who tremble at My word."

ISAIAH 66:2 NLT

"He who is greatest among you shall be your servant. And whoever exalts himself will be humbled, and he who humbles himself will be exalted."

MATTHEW 23:11-12 NKJV

"Truly, I say to you, unless you turn and become like children, you will never enter the kingdom of heaven. Whoever humbles himself like this child is the greatest in the kingdom of heaven."

MATTHEW 18:3-4 ESV

Pride leads to disgrace, but with humility comes wisdom.

PROVERBS 11:2 NLT

He has shown you, O mortal, what is good. And what does the LORD require of you? To act justly and to love mercy and to walk humbly with your God.

MICAH 6:8 NIV

A man's pride will bring him low, but the humble in spirit will retain honor.

PROVERBS 29:23 NKJV

Do nothing out of selfish ambition or vain conceit. Rather, in humility value others above yourselves, not looking to your own interests but each of you to the interests of the others.

PHILIPPIANS 2:3-4 NIV

The LORD supports the humble, but He brings the wicked down into the dust.

PSALM 147:6 NLT

"Blessed are the poor in spirit, for theirs is the kingdom of heaven."

MATTHEW 5:3 NKJV

Haughtiness goes before destruction; humility precedes honor.

PROVERBS 18:12 NLT

Be like-minded, be sympathetic, love one another, be compassionate and humble.

1 PETER 3:8 NIV

"If My people who are called by My name will humble themselves, and pray and seek My face, and turn from their wicked ways, then I will hear from heaven, and will forgive their sin and heal their land."

2 CHRONICLES 7:14 NKJV

"For all those who exalt themselves will be humbled, and those who humble themselves will be exalted."

LUKE 14:11 NIV

The meek will inherit the land and enjoy peace and prosperity.

PSALM 37:11 NIV

THE WORD
OF GOD
IS ALIVE
AND ACTIVE.
SHARPER
— THAN ANY —
DOUBLE-EDGED
SWORD.
HEBREWS 4:12

THE LIVING WORD

If you are having problems with your Bible study, it might be worthwhile to consider that perhaps you are spending more time reading *about* God than spending time *with* God.

It is necessary to know the Incarnate Word personally. In order to know Him you have to reach out to Him in the silence of your inner room through contemplation and prayer. If you draw near to God in this manner, you will find that the Word starts to assume new life and meaning, because you are no longer merely reading a book. Instead you are *living* the Word together with its Author!

Incarnate Word of God, I open myself to You, so that You can fill me with Your Spirit and Your Word, and truly live in me.

AMEN.

All Scripture is inspired by God and is useful to teach us what is true and to make us realize what is wrong in our lives. It corrects us when we are wrong and teaches us to do what is right. God uses it to prepare and equip His people to do every good work.

---

2 TIMOTHY 3:16-17 NLT

Above all, you must understand that no prophecy of Scripture came about by the prophet's own interpretation of things. For prophecy never had its origin in the human will, but prophets, though human, spoke from God as they were carried along by the Holy Spirit.

---

2 PETER 1:20-21 NIV

"Heaven and earth will pass away, but My words will never pass away."

MATTHEW 24:35 NIV

Jesus answered, "It is written: 'Man shall not live on bread alone, but on every word that comes from the mouth of God.'"

MATTHEW 4:4 NIV

For whatever was written in former days was written for our instruction, that through endurance and through the encouragement of the Scriptures we might have hope.

ROMANS 15:4 ESV

Don't just listen to God's word. You must do what it says. Otherwise, you are only fooling yourselves. For if you listen to the word and don't obey, it is like glancing at your face in a mirror. You see yourself, walk away, and forget what you look like. But if you look carefully into the perfect law that sets you free, and if you do what it says and don't forget what you heard, then God will bless you for doing it.

JAMES 1:22-25 NLT

The Word became flesh and made His dwelling among us.

JOHN 1:14 NIV

The entirety of Your word is truth, and every one of Your righteous judgments endures forever.

PSALM 119:160 NKJV

"Blessed rather are those who hear the word of God and obey it."

LUKE 11:28 NIV

"Everyone then who hears these words of Mine and does them will be like a wise man who built his house on the rock. And the rain fell, and the floods came, and the winds blew and beat on that house, but it did not fall, because it had been founded on the rock. And everyone who hears these words of Mine and does not do them will be like a foolish man who built his house on the sand. And the rain fell, and the floods came, and the winds blew and beat against that house, and it fell, and great was the fall of it."

MATTHEW 7:24-27 ESV

Your word, LORD, is eternal; it stands firm in the heavens.

PSALM 119:89 NIV

In the beginning was the Word, and the Word was with God, and the Word was God.

JOHN 1:1 ESV

Blessed are those whose way is blameless, who walk in the law of the LORD! Blessed are those who keep His testimonies, who seek Him with their whole heart, who also do no wrong, but walk in His ways!

PSALM 119:1-3 ESV

The grass withers and the flowers fade beneath the breath of the LORD. And so it is with people. The grass withers and the flowers fade, but the word of our God stands forever.

ISAIAH 40:7-8 NLT

As the Scriptures say, "People are like grass; their beauty is like a flower in the field. The grass withers and the flower fades. But the word of the Lord remains forever." And that word is the Good News that was preached to you.

---

1 PETER 1:24-25 NLT

"Keep this Book of the Law always on your lips; meditate on it day and night, so that you may be careful to do everything written in it. Then you will be prosperous and successful."

JOSHUA 1:8 NIV

SET YOUR MINDS
ON THINGS
ABOVE,
— NOT ON —
EARTHLY THINGS.

COLOSSIANS 3:2

KEEP YOUR EYES ON JESUS

When talking about everything Jesus has done for them, many believers turn the spotlight on themselves instead of on Jesus Christ. Without noticing it, this egotistical attitude becomes part of their lives and it is detrimental to their spiritual experiences as disciples of Christ.

No matter how wonderful your own spiritual experiences might be, they can only be credible if Jesus is the focal point.

Lord Jesus, I keep You at the center of my life, because when I have You, I have everything.

AMEN.

Blessed are those who keep His statutes and seek Him with all their heart.

PSALM 119:2 NIV

Test all things; hold fast what is good.

1 THESSALONIANS 5:21 NKJV

You will keep in perfect peace those whose minds are steadfast, because they trust in You.

ISAIAH 26:3 NIV

Those who live according to the flesh set their minds on the things of the flesh, but those who live according to the Spirit, the things of the Spirit.

ROMANS 8:5 NKJV

Let your eyes look straight ahead; fix your gaze directly before you.

PROVERBS 4:25 NIV

Blessed is the man who walks not in the counsel of the wicked, nor stands in the way of sinners, nor sits in the seat of scoffers; but his delight is in the law of the LORD, and on his law he meditates day and night.

PSALM 1:1-2 ESV

Fix your thoughts on what is true, and honorable, and right, and pure, and lovely, and admirable. Think about things that are excellent and worthy of praise.

PHILIPPIANS 4:8 NLT

Do your best to present yourself to God as one approved, a worker who has no need to be ashamed, rightly handling the word of truth.

---

2 TIMOTHY 2:15 ESV

"No one can serve two masters; for either he will hate the one and love the other, or else he will be loyal to the one and despise the other. You cannot serve God and mammon."

MATTHEW 6:24 NKJV

Tune your ears to wisdom, and concentrate on understanding. Cry out for insight, and ask for understanding. Search for them as you would for silver; seek them like hidden treasures. Then you will understand what it means to fear the LORD, and you will gain knowledge of God.

PROVERBS 2:2-5 NLT

My voice You shall hear in the morning, O LORD; in the morning I will direct it to You, and I will look up.

PSALM 5:3 NKJV

God looks down from heaven on the entire human race; He looks to see if anyone is truly wise, if anyone seeks God.

PSALM 53:2 NLT

Unto You I lift up my eyes, O You who dwell in the heavens. Behold, as the eyes of servants look to the hand of their masters, as the eyes of a maid to the hand of her mistress, so our eyes look to the LORD our God.

PSALM 123:1-2 NKJV

Sensible people keep their eyes glued on wisdom, but a fool's eyes wander to the ends of the earth.

PROVERBS 17:24 NLT

"Listen to Me, you who pursue righteousness, you who seek the LORD: look to the rock from which you were hewn, and to the quarry from which you were dug."

ISAIAH 51:1 ESV

Sow righteousness for yourselves, reap the fruit of unfailing love, and break up your unplowed ground; for it is time to seek the LORD, until He comes and showers His righteousness on you.

HOSEA 10:12 NIV

DON'T COPY THE
BEHAVIOR
AND CUSTOMS
OF THIS WORLD,
BUT LET
GOD TRANSFORM
YOU INTO A
NEW PERSON
BY CHANGING
THE WAY YOU THINK.

ROMANS 12:2

A RADICAL CHANGE

When you accept Christ as your Savior, things change because a radical change has taken place in your life. Through Jesus Christ, God reconciles us with Himself, by forgiving all our sins and declaring that we have been justified. Everything in our lives changes drastically. We live and do differently because Christ entered our lives.

This is what conversion actually means. It is like a beautiful stained-glass window that has been shattered. The Master Artist takes the fragments of our old sinful life and repairs it, turning it into something new and beautiful.

Savior, thank You for changing me and the way my life was to something far better.

AMEN.

If anyone is in Christ, the new creation has come: The old has gone, the new is here!

---

2 CORINTHIANS 5:17 NIV

Put on your new nature, and be renewed as you learn to know your Creator and become like Him.

COLOSSIANS 3:10 NLT

You were taught, with regard to your former way of life, to put off your old self, which is being corrupted by its deceitful desires; to be made new in the attitude of your minds; and to put on the new self, created to be like God in true righteousness and holiness.

EPHESIANS 4:22-24 NIV

In all circumstances take up the shield of faith, with which you can extinguish all the flaming darts of the evil one; and take the helmet of salvation, and the sword of the Spirit, which is the word of God, praying at all times in the Spirit, with all prayer and supplication. To that end keep alert with all perseverance, making supplication for all the saints.

EPHESIANS 6:16-18 ESV

Submit yourselves, then, to God. Resist the devil, and he will flee from you.

JAMES 4:7 NIV

Do not let any part of your body become an instrument of evil to serve sin. Instead, give yourselves completely to God, for you were dead, but now you have new life. So use your whole body as an instrument to do what is right for the glory of God. Sin is no longer your master, for you no longer live under the requirements of the law. Instead, you live under the freedom of God's grace.

ROMANS 6:13-14 NLT

Are we to continue in sin that grace may abound? By no means! How can we who died to sin still live in it? Do you not know that all of us who have been baptized into Christ Jesus were baptized into His death? We were buried therefore with Him by baptism into death, in order that, just as Christ was raised from the dead by the glory of the Father, we too might walk in newness of life.

ROMANS 6:1-4 ESV

When He died, He died once to break the power of sin. But now that He lives, He lives for the glory of God. So you also should consider yourselves to be dead to the power of sin and alive to God through Christ Jesus. Do not let sin control the way you live; do not give in to sinful desires.

ROMANS 6:10-12 NLT

Fight the good fight for the true faith. Hold tightly to the eternal life to which God has called you, which you have confessed so well before many witnesses. And I charge you before God, who gives life to all, and before Christ Jesus, who gave a good testimony before Pontius Pilate, that you obey this command without wavering. Then no one can find fault with you from now until our Lord Jesus Christ comes again.

---

1 TIMOTHY 6:12-14 NLT

Make it your goal to live a quiet life, minding your own business and working with your hands, just as we instructed you before. Then people who are not Christians will respect the way you live, and you will not need to depend on others.

---

1 THESSALONIANS 4:11-12 NLT

Rejoice always, pray without ceasing, in everything give thanks; for this is the will of God in Christ Jesus for you.

---

1 THESSALONIANS 5:16-18 NKJV

No temptation has overtaken you that is not common to man. God is faithful, and He will not let you be tempted beyond your ability, but with the temptation He will also provide the way of escape, that you may be able to endure it.

---

1 CORINTHIANS 10:13 ESV

The night is almost gone; the day of salvation will soon be here. So remove your dark deeds like dirty clothes, and put on the shining armor of right living.

ROMANS 13:12 NLT

Prove by the way you live that you have repented of your sins and turned to God.

MATTHEW 3:8 NLT

OUR GOD

IS A

GOD WHO SAVES!

THE SOVEREIGN

LORD

RESCUES US.

PSALM 68:20

SALVATION
THROUGH THE CROSS

There is salvation through the cross because Jesus died on it for the sins of all of mankind. We don't honor the cross, but the Man who died on it and opened up the path to heaven and the loving heart of God. We are again reconciled with God.

The message to us all is: Salvation comes through the cross.

Crucified and risen Savior, grant that I will never boast except in the cross of Jesus. By Your death on the cross, salvation came for me too.

AMEN.

"Most assuredly, I say to you, I am the door of the sheep. All who ever came before Me are thieves and robbers, but the sheep did not hear them. I am the door. If anyone enters by Me, he will be saved, and will go in and out and find pasture. The thief does not come except to steal, and to kill, and to destroy. I have come that they may have life, and that they may have it more abundantly."

JOHN 10:7-10 NKJV

In Him we have redemption through His blood, the forgiveness of sins, in accordance with the riches of God's grace that He lavished on us.

EPHESIANS 1:7-8 NIV

It is good that one should hope and wait quietly for the salvation of the LORD.

LAMENTATIONS 3:26 NKJV

The LORD takes pleasure in His people; He will beautify the humble with salvation.

PSALM 149:4 NKJV

Restore to me the joy of Your salvation and grant me a willing spirit, to sustain me.

PSALM 51:12 NIV

Jesus is the stone that was rejected by you, the builders, which has become the cornerstone. And there is salvation in no one else, for there is no other name under heaven given among men by which we must be saved."

ACTS 4:11-12 ESV

"I tell you the truth, those who listen to My message and believe in God who sent Me have eternal life. They will never be condemned for their sins, but they have already passed from death into life."

JOHN 5:24 NLT

"My sheep hear My voice, and I know them, and they follow Me. And I give them eternal life, and they shall never perish; neither shall anyone snatch them out of My hand. My Father, who has given them to Me, is greater than all; and no one is able to snatch them out of My Father's hand."

JOHN 10:27-29 NKJV

"All those the Father gives Me will come to Me, and whoever comes to Me I will never drive away. For I have come down from heaven not to do My will but to do the will of Him who sent Me. And this is the will of Him who sent Me, that I shall lose none of all those He has given Me, but raise them up at the last day."

JOHN 6:37-39 NIV

For there is no distinction between Jew and Greek, for the same Lord over all is rich to all who call upon Him. For "whoever calls on the name of the LORD shall be saved."

ROMANS 10:12-13 NKJV

I delight greatly in the LORD; my soul rejoices in my God. For He has clothed me with garments of salvation and arrayed me in a robe of righteousness.

ISAIAH 61:10 NIV

Believe in the Lord Jesus, and you will be saved, you and your household.

ACTS 16:31 ESV

If you openly declare that Jesus is Lord and believe in your heart that God raised Him from the dead, you will be saved. For it is by believing in your heart that you are made right with God, and it is by openly declaring your faith that you are saved.

ROMANS 10:9-10 NLT

He is able to save to the uttermost those who draw near to God through Him, since He always lives to make intercession for them.

HEBREWS 7:25 ESV

God says, "At just the right time, I heard you. On the day of salvation, I helped you." Indeed, the "right time" is now. Today is the day of salvation.

---

2 CORINTHIANS 6:2 NLT

If we walk in the light, as He is in the light, we have fellowship with one another, and the blood of Jesus, His Son, cleanses us from all sin.

---

1 JOHN 1:7 NIV

Our help

is from

The Lord,

who made

heaven

and earth.

Psalm 124:8

HELP

IN THE MIDST OF CRISES

God did not promise us a life of eternal happiness on earth or a problem-free existence, but He did promise that in the stillness and in the darkness He will be with us and He will help us.

It is highly unlikely that you will have a problem-free life; in fact, you can probably count on the fact that problems and crises will cross your path, but in the midst of those crises you need never be worried. After all, you have the promise that God will never let you down, that He will be with you to lead you, help you and strengthen you.

Heavenly Father, it is wonderful that You have promised to be with me, to strengthen me and to help me, to hold me tight and to save me. I come now to lay claim to that promise!

AMEN.

I will lift up my eyes to the hills – from whence comes my help? My help comes from the LORD, who made heaven and earth.

PSALM 121:1-2 NKJV

The LORD is my strength and my shield; in Him my heart trusts, and I am helped; my heart exults, and with my song I give thanks to Him.

PSALM 28:7 ESV

Those who look to Him for help will be radiant with joy; no shadow of shame will darken their faces.

PSALM 34:5 NLT

We may boldly say: "The LORD is my helper; I will not fear. What can man do to me?"

HEBREWS 13:6 NKJV

Our help is from the LORD, who made heaven and earth.

PSALM 124:8 NLT

Joyful are those who have the God of Israel as their helper, whose hope is in the LORD their God.

PSALM 146:5 NLT

Likewise the Spirit also helps in our weaknesses. For we do not know what we should pray for as we ought, but the Spirit Himself makes intercession for us with groanings which cannot be uttered.

ROMANS 8:26 NKJV

I will be fully satisfied as with the richest of foods; with singing lips my mouth will praise You. Because You are my help, I sing in the shadow of Your wings.

PSALM 63:5, 7 NIV

You are from God and have overcome them, for He who is in you is greater than he who is in the world.

---

1 JOHN 4:4 ESV

Surely God is my help; the Lord is the one who sustains me.

PSALM 54:4 NIV

The Lord is for me; He will help me. I will look in triumph at those who hate me. It is better to take refuge in the Lord than to trust in people.

PSALM 118:7-8 NLT

He will deliver the needy when he cries, the poor also, and him who has no helper.

PSALM 72:12 NKJV

As for me, I am poor and needy; may the Lord think of me. You are my help and my deliverer; You are my God, do not delay.

PSALM 40:17 NIV

"The Helper, the Holy Spirit, whom the Father will send in My name, He will teach you all things, and bring to your remembrance all things that I said to you."

JOHN 14:26 NKJV

The righteous person faces many troubles, but the Lord comes to the rescue each time.

PSALM 34:19 NLT

"I tell you the truth: it is to your advantage that I go away, for if I do not go away, the Helper will not come to you. But if I go, I will send Him to you."

JOHN 16:7 ESV

I will praise Your name, LORD, for it is good. You have delivered me from all my troubles, and my eyes have looked in triumph on my foes.

PSALM 54:6-7 NIV

The LORD rescues the godly; He is their fortress in times of trouble. The LORD helps them, rescuing them from the wicked.

PSALM 37:39-40 NLT

The LORD will fight for you, and you have only to be silent.

EXODUS 14:14 ESV

The angel of the LORD is a guard; He surrounds and defends all who fear Him.

PSALM 34:7 NLT

THE NAME OF
THE LORD
IS A
FORTIFIED TOWER;
THE RIGHTEOUS
RUN TO IT
AND ARE SAFE.
PROVERBS 18:10

THE NAME ABOVE ALL NAMES

In your life, there are times when anxiety rises within your soul. Your inner sanctuary is the place where you can go to pour out your heart before God. Be assured of this: only the unfailing love of God has an answer for the cry of desperation of a suffering soul. Because He gave His eternal love for us – the image of the Father's glory!

And from us nothing more is required than to bow before the name above all names, Jesus the living Christ, our Redeemer and Savior. He delivers us out of every problem, even the greatest need of our heart and soul.

I praise and thank You, Lord Jesus, that
You gained mercy for me from God
through Your reconciling blood.

AMEN.

Everyone who calls on the name of the LORD will be saved.

ROMANS 10:13 NLT

Therefore, God elevated Him to the place of highest honor and gave Him the name above all other names, that at the name of Jesus every knee should bow, in heaven and on earth and under the earth, and every tongue confess that Jesus Christ is Lord, to the glory of God the Father.

PHILIPPIANS 2:9-11 NLT

"Whatever you ask in My name, this I will do, that the Father may be glorified in the Son. If you ask Me anything in My name, I will do it."

JOHN 14:13-14 ESV

You were cleansed; you were made holy; you were made right with God by calling on the name of the Lord Jesus Christ and by the Spirit of our God.

---

1 CORINTHIANS 6:11 NLT

"My name is honored by people of other nations from morning till night. All around the world they offer sweet incense and pure offerings in honor of My name. For My name is great among the nations," says the LORD of Heaven's Armies.

MALACHI 1:11 NLT

God said, "I AM WHO I AM." And He said, "Thus you shall say to the children of Israel, 'I AM has sent me to you.'"

EXODUS 3:14 NKJV

He is the One all the prophets testified about, saying that everyone who believes in Him will have their sins forgiven through His name.

ACTS 10:43 NLT

Sing to God, sing in praise of His name, extol Him who rides on the clouds; rejoice before Him – His name is the LORD.

PSALM 68:4 NIV

On His robe and on His thigh He has a name written, King of kings and Lord of lords.

REVELATION 19:16 ESV

"I am the Alpha and the Omega," says the Lord God, "who is, and who was, and who is to come, the Almighty."

REVELATION 1:8 NIV

There is none like You, O LORD; You are great, and Your name is great in might.

JEREMIAH 10:6 ESV

Repent and be baptized, every one of you, in the name of Jesus Christ for the forgiveness of your sins. And you will receive the gift of the Holy Spirit.

ACTS 2:38 NIV

And whatever you do, in word or deed, do everything in the name of the Lord Jesus, giving thanks to God the Father through Him.

COLOSSIANS 3:17 ESV

"I am the Alpha and the Omega, the First and the Last, the Beginning and the End."

REVELATION 22:13 NLT

LET

LOVE

BE YOUR

HIGHEST GOAL!

1 CORINTHIANS 14:1

AN EXAMPLE OF STRENGTH THROUGH LOVE

The sad fact is that we live in a world where corruption, scandal and violence are the order of the day. The normal human reaction to this is to fight fire with fire. However, the only way to handle evil is through the path of divine love.

Love is not a sign of weakness, as some would have you believe. If we consider Christ's courage and endurance on the cross, nobody can dare to call Him weak. As it was then, so it is now: only the forgiving love of Christ can and will conquer the powers of evil.

Father God, You are love. This is clearly spelt out on the Cross.

AMEN.

"I am giving you a new commandment: Love each other. Just as I have loved you, you should love each other."

JOHN 13:34 NLT

We love because He first loved us. Whoever claims to love God yet hates a brother or sister is a liar. For whoever does not love their brother and sister, whom they have seen, cannot love God, whom they have not seen. And He has given us this command: Anyone who loves God must also love their brother and sister.

1 JOHN 4:19-21 NIV

Love prospers when a fault is forgiven, but dwelling on it separates close friends.

PROVERBS 17:9 NLT

There is no fear in love; but perfect love casts out fear.

1 JOHN 4:18 NKJV

"Love your neighbor as yourself."

LEVITICUS 19:18 NIV

Let love and faithfulness never leave you; bind them around your neck, write them on the tablet of your heart.

PROVERBS 3:3 NIV

Whoever pursues righteousness and unfailing love will find life, righteousness, and honor.

PROVERBS 21:21 NLT

Love is patient, love is kind. It does not envy, it does not boast, it is not proud.

---

1 CORINTHIANS 13:4 NIV

Do everything in love.

---

1 CORINTHIANS 16:14 NIV

This is love: not that we loved God, but that He loved us and sent His Son as an atoning sacrifice for our sins.

---

1 JOHN 4:10 NIV

Live a life filled with love, following the example of Christ. He loved us and offered Himself as a sacrifice for us, a pleasing aroma to God.

EPHESIANS 5:2 NLT

Love the LORD your God with all your heart and with all your soul and with all your strength.

DEUTERONOMY 6:5 NIV

If we love each other, God lives in us, and His love is brought to full expression in us.

---

1 JOHN 4:12 NLT

Love never fails.

---

1 CORINTHIANS 13:8 NKJV

These three remain: faith, hope and love. But the greatest of these is love.

---

1 CORINTHIANS 13:13 NIV

Love covers over a multitude of sins.

---

1 PETER 4:8 NIV

"The one who loves Me will be loved by My Father, and I too will love them and show Myself to them."

JOHN 14:21 NIV

TRUE GODLINESS

WITH

CONTENTMENT

IS ITSELF

GREAT WEALTH.

1 TIMOTHY 6:6

CONTENTMENT
IN ALL CIRCUMSTANCES

Learn to be content with the things you have, and be thankful for them. Don't accept unpleasant conditions as permanent, but in the meantime learn to rejoice and be content. The alternative is that you will always be hounded by fear, because ingratitude leads to fear and anxiety.

Be thankful for what God has given you and don't complain about the shortcomings in your life. Don't see only the negative things around you; see the goodness and grace of the Lord instead. That is how you are set free from fear.

Lord Jesus, even if I go through dark depths, I will not fear, because I am thankful that You are with me.

AMEN.

The righteous eat to their hearts' content, but the stomach of the wicked goes hungry.

PROVERBS 13:25 NIV

For we brought nothing into this world, and it is certain we can carry nothing out. And having food and clothing, with these we shall be content.

1 TIMOTHY 6:7-8 NKJV

Those who love money will never have enough. How meaningless to think that wealth brings true happiness!

ECCLESIASTES 5:10 NLT

Enjoy what you have rather than desiring what you don't have. Just dreaming about nice things is meaningless—like chasing the wind.

ECCLESIASTES 6:9 NLT

Keep your lives free from the love of money and be content with what you have, because God has said, "Never will I leave you; never will I forsake you."

HEBREWS 13:5 NIV

"Beware! Guard against every kind of greed. Life is not measured by how much you own."

LUKE 12:15 NLT

I have learned in whatever situation I am to be content. I know how to be brought low, and I know how to abound. In any and every circumstance, I have learned the secret of facing plenty and hunger, abundance and need.

PHILIPPIANS 4:11-12 ESV

I am content with weaknesses, insults, hardships, persecutions, and calamities. For when I am weak, then I am strong.

---

2 CORINTHIANS 12:10 ESV

Remove falsehood and lies far from me; give me neither poverty nor riches – feed me with the food allotted to me; lest I be full and deny You, and say, "Who is the LORD?" Or lest I be poor and steal, and profane the name of my God.

PROVERBS 30:8-9 NKJV

A greedy man stirs up strife, but the one who trusts in the LORD will be enriched.

PROVERBS 28:25 ESV

Better to have little, with godliness, than to be rich and dishonest.

PROVERBS 16:8 NLT

Command those who are rich in this present age not to be haughty, nor to trust in uncertain riches but in the living God, who gives us richly all things to enjoy. Let them do good, that they be rich in good works, ready to give, willing to share, storing up for themselves a good foundation for the time to come, that they may lay hold on eternal life.

---

1 TIMOTHY 6:17-19 NKJV

The backslider in heart will be filled with the fruit of his ways, and a good man will be filled with the fruit of his ways.

PROVERBS 14:14 ESV

Better the little that the righteous have than the wealth of many wicked.

PSALM 37:16 NIV

A sound heart is life to the body, but envy is rottenness to the bones.

PROVERBS 14:30 NKJV

The LORD is my shepherd; I shall not want. He makes me lie down in green pastures. He leads me beside still waters.

PSALM 23:1-2 ESV

TEACH US
TO NUMBER
OUR DAYS,
THAT WE
MAY GAIN
A HEART
OF WISDOM.

PSALM 90:12

USING YOUR TIME WISELY

One of the great dangers of faith is that we will become so relaxed in the unending grace of God that we think any time that suits us will be good enough for allowing God into our lives.

Jesus told many parables about the land owner who returned suddenly and his servants found themselves in a difficult position because they thought that he would return later. Our God is the God who unexpectedly intervenes in situations. God might come at any time! Are you ready for Him?

Father God, in the Bible You warn that You will be coming quickly. Prepare us for that day. Help us to use our time wisely and to not become too relaxed.

AMEN.

Be very careful, then, how you live – not as unwise but as wise, making the most of every opportunity, because the days are evil.

EPHESIANS 5:15-16 NIV

Those who obey him will not be punished. Those who are wise will find a time and a way to do what is right.

ECCLESIASTES 8:5 NLT

Since his days are determined, and the number of his months is with You, and You have appointed his limits that he cannot pass, look away from him and leave him alone, that he may enjoy, like a hired hand, his day. For there is hope for a tree, if it be cut down, that it will sprout again, and that its shoots will not cease.

JOB 14:5-7 ESV

Be wise in the way you act toward outsiders; make the most of every opportunity.

COLOSSIANS 4:5 NIV

"We must quickly carry out the tasks assigned us by the One who sent us. The night is coming, and then no one can work."

JOHN 9:4 NLT

Our days may come to seventy years, or eighty, if our strength endures; yet the best of them are but trouble and sorrow, for they quickly pass, and we fly away.

PSALM 90:10 NIV

My child, listen to me and do as I say, and you will have a long, good life.

PROVERBS 4:10 NLT

Now listen, you who say, "Today or tomorrow we will go to this or that city, spend a year there, carry on business and make money." Why, you do not even know what will happen tomorrow. What is your life? You are a mist that appears for a little while and then vanishes. Instead, you ought to say, "If it is the Lord's will, we will live and do this or that."

JAMES 4:13-15 NIV

The LORD keeps you from all harm and watches over your life. The LORD keeps watch over you as you come and go, both now and forever.

PSALM 121:7-8 NLT

Listen, I tell you a mystery: We will not all sleep, but we will all be changed – in a flash, in the twinkling of an eye, at the last trumpet.

---

1 CORINTHIANS 15:51-52 NIV

Anyone who belongs to Christ has become a new person. The old life is gone; a new life has begun!

---

2 CORINTHIANS 5:17 NLT

LORD, make me to know my end, and what is the measure of my days, that I may know how frail I am. Indeed, You have made my days as handbreadths, and my age is as nothing before You; certainly every man at his best state is but vapor. Surely every man walks about like a shadow; surely they busy themselves in vain; he heaps up riches, and does not know who will gather them. And now, Lord, what do I wait for? My hope is in You.

PSALM 39:4-7 NKJV

You see me when I travel and when I rest at home. You know everything I do. You know what I am going to say even before I say it, LORD. You go before me and follow me. You place Your hand of blessing on my head.

PSALM 139:3-5 NLT

Whether you eat or drink or whatever you do, do it all for the glory of God.

---

1 CORINTHIANS 10:31 NIV

I concluded there is nothing better than to be happy and enjoy ourselves as long as we can. And people should eat and drink and enjoy the fruits of their labor, for these are gifts from God.

ECCLESIASTES 3:12-13 NLT

For everything there is a season, and a time for every matter under heaven: a time to be born, and a time to die; a time to plant, and a time to pluck up what is planted.

ECCLESIASTES 3:1-2 ESV

JESUS CHRIST

IS THE

SAME YESTERDAY

AND TODAY

AND FOREVER.

HEBREWS 13:8

AN EVER-CHANGING WORLD

There is no doubt that in this life you will be confronted by change. Some changes you will reject and others you will accept. Some will threaten your faith, but if you hold on to the promise that the eternal Father never changes, you will survive and even be enriched by new and stimulating ideas.

In the steadfast knowledge of the unfailing truth that the eternal God is also eternally present in your life, you can evaluate every change in light of the knowledge that He gives to you. Then you can be assured that He will guide you on the path of truth in the midst of an ever-changing world.

O Lord, who never changes, stay with me!

AMEN.

"I am the Alpha and the Omega, the Beginning and the End, the First and the Last."

REVELATION 22:13 NKJV

Have you not known? Have you not heard? The LORD is the everlasting God, the Creator of the ends of the earth.

ISAIAH 40:28 ESV

LORD, You remain the same forever! Your throne continues from generation to generation.

LAMENTATIONS 5:19 NLT

"I alone am God! I am God, and there is none like Me. Only I can tell you the future before it even happens. Everything I plan will come to pass, for I do whatever I wish. I will call a swift bird of prey from the east – a leader from a distant land to come and do My bidding. I have said what I would do, and I will do it."

ISAIAH 46:9-11 NLT

The grass withers and the flowers fall, but the word of our God endures forever.

ISAIAH 40:8 NIV

God is not human, that He should lie, not a human being, that He should change His mind. Does He speak and then not act? Does He promise and not fulfill?

NUMBERS 23:19 NIV

"You, Lord, laid the foundation of the earth in the beginning, and the heavens are the work of Your hands; they will perish, but You remain; they will all wear out like a garment, like a robe You will roll them up, like a garment they will be changed. But You are the same, and Your years will have no end."

HEBREWS 1:10-12 ESV

Whatever is good and perfect is a gift coming down to us from God our Father, who created all the lights in the heavens. He never changes or casts a shifting shadow.

JAMES 1:17 NLT

Your kingdom is an everlasting kingdom, and Your dominion endures throughout all generations.

PSALM 145:13 ESV

Of old You laid the foundation of the earth, and the heavens are the work of Your hands. They will perish, but You will endure; yes, they will all grow old like a garment; like a cloak You will change them, and they will be changed. But You are the same, and Your years will have no end.

PSALM 102:25-27 NKJV

Your word, LORD, is eternal; it stands firm in the heavens. Your faithfulness continues through all generations; You established the earth, and it endures. Your laws endure to this day, for all things serve You.

PSALM 119:89-91 NIV

Lord, through all the generations You have been our home! Before the mountains were born, before You gave birth to the earth and the world, from beginning to end, You are God.

PSALM 90:1-2 NLT

The plans of the LORD stand firm forever, the purposes of his heart through all generations.

PSALM 33:11 NIV

Give thanks to the Lord, for He is good! Give thanks to the God of gods. Give thanks to the Lord of lords. His faithful love endures forever.

PSALM 136:1-3 NLT

If we are unfaithful, He remains faithful, for He cannot deny who He is.

---

2 TIMOTHY 2:13 NLT

He who is the Glory of Israel does not lie or change His mind; for He is not a human being, that He should change His mind.

---

1 SAMUEL 15:29 NIV

— As far as —

THE EAST IS

FROM THE WEST,

SO FAR HAS

HE REMOVED

OUR TRANSGRESSIONS

FROM US.

Psalm 103:12

THE ULTIMATE

FORGIVENESS

God's attitude toward you is one of total acceptance, forgiveness and sincere love. There is no condemnation for those who are in Christ. So you don't need to torture yourself with thoughts of unworthiness. You don't need to be defeated by fear, problems or circumstances. God expects you to believe His Word about yourself.

Lead a life controlled by the Spirit, resist sin and walk in righteousness. Live in His power and victory; know His love, acceptance and forgiveness. Look at others and yourself through His eyes.

Lord, I have received forgiveness, and in gratitude, I sing a song of salvation.

AMEN.

"I have blotted out, like a thick cloud, your transgressions, and like a cloud, your sins. Return to Me, for I have redeemed you."

ISAIAH 44:22 NKJV

"I will forgive their wickedness, and I will never again remember their sins."

HEBREWS 8:12 NLT

"Though your sins are like scarlet, they shall be as white as snow; though they are red as crimson, they shall be like wool."

ISAIAH 1:18 NIV

We praise God for the glorious grace He has poured out on us who belong to His dear Son. He is so rich in kindness and grace that He purchased our freedom with the blood of His Son and forgave our sins.

EPHESIANS 1:6-7 NLT

All the prophets testify about Him that everyone who believes in Him receives forgiveness of sins through His name.

ACTS 10:43 NIV

Now there is no condemnation for those who belong to Christ Jesus. And because you belong to Him, the power of the life-giving Spirit has freed you from the power of sin that leads to death.

ROMANS 8:1-2 NLT

If anyone sins, we have an Advocate with the Father, Jesus Christ the righteous. And He Himself is the propitiation for our sins, and not for ours only but also for the whole world.

---

1 JOHN 2:1-2 NKJV

The Lord our God is merciful and forgiving.

DANIEL 9:9 NLT

Who is a God like You, who pardons sin and forgives the transgression of the remnant of His inheritance? You do not stay angry forever but delight to show mercy. You will again have compassion on us; You will tread our sins underfoot and hurl all our iniquities into the depths of the sea.

MICAH 7:18-19 NIV

"Be encouraged, My child! Your sins are forgiven."

MATTHEW 9:2 NLT

It is the power of God that brings salvation to everyone who believes.

ROMANS 1:16 NIV

He has delivered us from the domain of darkness and transferred us to the kingdom of His beloved Son, in whom we have redemption, the forgiveness of sins.

COLOSSIANS 1:13-14 ESV

The LORD is my light and my salvation – whom shall I fear? The LORD is the stronghold of my life – of whom shall I be afraid?

PSALM 27:1 NIV

If we confess our sins to Him, He is faithful and just to forgive us our sins and to cleanse us from all wickedness.

---

1 JOHN 1:9 NLT

The LORD is the strength of His people, a fortress of salvation for His anointed one. Save Your people and bless Your inheritance; be their Shepherd and carry them forever.

PSALM 28:8-9 NIV

Christ was offered once for all time as a sacrifice to take away the sins of many people. He will come again, not to deal with our sins, but to bring salvation to all who are eagerly waiting for Him.

HEBREWS 9:28 NLT

For the
WAGES OF SIN
is death,
but the
FREE GIFT OF GOD
IS ETERNAL LIFE
through
Christ Jesus
OUR LORD.
Romans 6:23

PLANNING FOR

ETERNITY

It is astonishing that intelligent people seriously consider the development of their earthly plans, but pay no attention to the time when they will leave this world and step into eternity.

To survey life with a sense of eternity is to give new perspective to your daily life. You ought to perform your daily task to the honor of God and should live your entire life so that it is acceptable to Him. To stand in the doorway of the spiritual life and place your hands with love in the hands of God, is the soul-enriching culmination of this life.

Risen Savior, I place my life and welfare in Your faithful care and step into the unknown future with confidence.

AMEN.

"Truly, truly, I say to you, whoever believes has eternal life."

JOHN 6:47 ESV

"Everyone who lives in Me and believes in Me will never ever die."

JOHN 11:26 NLT

Whoever has the Son has life; whoever does not have the Son of God does not have life.

---

1 JOHN 5:12 ESV

"I give them eternal life, and they shall never perish; no one will snatch them out of My hand. My Father, who has given them to Me, is greater than all; no one can snatch them out of My Father's hand. I and the Father are one."

JOHN 10:28-30 NIV

"My Father's will is that everyone who looks to the Son and believes in Him shall have eternal life."

JOHN 6:40 NIV

"Indeed, the time is coming when all the dead in their graves will hear the voice of God's Son, and they will rise again. Those who have done good will rise to experience eternal life, and those who have continued in evil will rise to experience judgment."

JOHN 5:28-29 NLT

Therefore we do not lose heart. Even though our outward man is perishing, yet the inward man is being renewed day by day. For our light affliction, which is but for a moment, is working for us a far more exceeding and eternal weight of glory.

2 CORINTHIANS 4:16-17 NKJV

I write these things to you who believe in the name of the Son of God so that you may know that you have eternal life.

---

1 JOHN 5:13 NIV

"For God so loved the world that He gave His only begotten Son, that whoever believes in Him should not perish but have everlasting life."

JOHN 3:16 NKJV

"You can enter God's Kingdom only through the narrow gate. The highway to hell is broad, and its gate is wide for the many who choose that way. But the gateway to life is very narrow and the road is difficult, and only a few ever find it."

MATTHEW 7:13-14 NLT

"Do not work for the food that perishes, but for the food that endures to eternal life, which the Son of Man will give to you. For on Him God the Father has set His seal."

JOHN 6:27 ESV

"Whoever drinks of this water will thirst again, but whoever drinks of the water that I shall give him will never thirst. But the water that I shall give him will become in him a fountain of water springing up into everlasting life."

JOHN 4:13-14 NKJV

"Father, the hour has come. Glorify Your Son, that Your Son may glorify You. For You granted Him authority over all people that He might give eternal life to all those You have given Him. Now this is eternal life: that they know You, the only true God, and Jesus Christ, whom You have sent."

JOHN 17:1-3 NIV

"If you refuse to take up your cross and follow Me, you are not worthy of being Mine. If you cling to your life, you will lose it; but if you give up your life for Me, you will find it."

MATTHEW 10:38-39 NLT

LET EVERYTHING
THAT HAS BREATH
PRAISE
THE LORD.
PRAISE THE LORD.
PSALM 150:6

GIVE GOD

THE GLORY

Don't pursue honor and glory for yourself. Don't strive to see your name prominently displayed when you have done something worthwhile for God. Give God the credit and glory.

Be prepared to stand aside and let other people praise God for what He did in and through you. Don't destroy Christ's work by your efforts to turn the spotlight on yourself. Thank the Lord that you were able to be involved and give Him all the honor and glory.

Lord my God, let the glory always go where it is due: to You.

AMEN.

Sing praises to God and to His name! Sing loud praises to Him who rides the clouds. His name is the LORD – rejoice in His presence!

PSALM 68:4 NLT

Praise be to the LORD God, the God of Israel, who alone does marvelous deeds. Praise be to His glorious name forever; may the whole earth be filled with His glory.

PSALM 72:18-19 NIV

I will praise the LORD according to His righteousness, and will sing praise to the name of the LORD Most High.

PSALM 7:17 NKJV

Praise the LORD! I will praise the LORD with my whole heart. The works of the LORD are great, studied by all who have pleasure in them. His work is honorable and glorious, and His righteousness endures forever.

PSALM 111:1-3 NKJV

Let them praise the name of the LORD, for His name alone is exalted; His majesty is above earth and heaven.

PSALM 148:13 ESV

Praise the LORD! Sing to the LORD a new song. Sing His praises in the assembly of the faithful.

PSALM 149:1 NLT

Declare His glory among the nations, His wonders among all peoples. For the LORD is great and greatly to be praised; He is also to be feared above all gods.

---

1 CHRONICLES 16:24-25 NKJV

Because Your steadfast love is better than life, my lips will praise You.

PSALM 63:3 ESV

LORD, You are my God. I will exalt You, I will praise Your name, for You have done wonderful things; Your counsels of old are faithfulness and truth.

ISAIAH 25:1 NKJV

With all my heart I will praise You, O Lord my God. I will give glory to Your name forever, for Your love for me is very great.

PSALM 86:12-13 NLT

Praise Him, you highest heavens, and you waters above the heavens! Let them praise the name of the LORD! For He commanded and they were created. And He established them forever and ever; He gave a decree, and it shall not pass away.

PSALM 148:4-6 ESV

Sing praises to God, sing praises! Sing praises to our King, sing praises! For God is the King of all the earth; sing praises with a psalm!

PSALM 47:6-7 ESV

Praise the LORD. Praise the LORD, you His servants; praise the name of the LORD. Let the name of the LORD be praised, both now and forevermore. From the rising of the sun to the place where it sets, the name of the LORD is to be praised.

PSALM 113:1-3 NIV

Shout to the LORD, all the earth; break out in praise and sing for joy!

PSALM 98:4 NLT

Praise the LORD, for the LORD is good; sing praises to His name, for it is pleasant.

PSALM 135:3 NKJV

I will praise the name of God with a song; I will magnify Him with thanksgiving.

PSALM 69:30 ESV

THE FEAR OF
THE LORD
IS THE
BEGINNING
OF WISDOM;
A GOOD
UNDERSTANDING
HAVE ALL
THOSE WHO DO
HIS COMMANDMENTS.

PSALM 111:10

REVERENCE
FOR THE LORD

When we serve the Lord in fear and trembling, it is a positive form of reverence and respect for God's greatness and majesty. This kind of fear is completely different to the fear that is a destructive and negative emotion and the result of transgression and sin. It keeps us inside God's directives so that we may lead a safer and blessed life.

The choice is yours. You either live in positive fear before God, or you live in fear and trembling in a place of sin and misery.

Loving Father God, I approach Your majesty in fear and trembling, but also with love.

AMEN.

Since we are receiving a Kingdom that is unshakable, let us be thankful and please God by worshiping Him with holy fear and awe. For our God is a devouring fire.

HEBREWS 12:28-29 NLT

Be sure to fear the LORD and serve Him faithfully with all your heart; consider what great things He has done for you.

---

1 SAMUEL 12:24 NIV

In mercy and truth atonement is provided for iniquity; and by the fear of the LORD one departs from evil.

PROVERBS 16:6 NKJV

"I tell you, My friends, do not be afraid of those who kill the body and after that can do no more. But I will show you whom you should fear: Fear Him who, after your body has been killed, has authority to throw you into hell. Yes, I tell you, fear Him."

LUKE 12:4-5 NIV

From the throne came a voice saying, "Praise our God, all you His servants, you who fear Him, small and great."

REVELATION 19:5 ESV

Honor all people. Love the brotherhood. Fear God.

1 PETER 2:17 NKJV

"Do not curse the deaf or put a stumbling block in front of the blind, but fear your God. I am the LORD."

LEVITICUS 19:14 NIV

How joyful are those who fear the LORD – all who follow His ways! You will enjoy the fruit of your labor. How joyful and prosperous you will be!

PSALM 128:1-2 NLT

Reverence for the Lord is pure, lasting forever. The laws of the Lord are true; each one is fair.

PSALM 19:9 NLT

The Lord takes pleasure in those who fear Him, in those who hope in His steadfast love.

PSALM 147:11 ESV

The angel of the Lord encamps all around those who fear Him, and delivers them.

PSALM 34:7 NKJV

Whoever fears the Lord has a secure fortress, and for their children it will be a refuge. The fear of the Lord is a fountain of life, turning a person from the snares of death.

PROVERBS 14:26-27 NIV

Fear God and keep His commandments, for this is the whole duty of man.

ECCLESIASTES 12:13 ESV

Let the whole world fear the LORD, and let everyone stand in awe of Him. For when He spoke, the world began! It appeared at His command.

PSALM 33:8-9 NLT

The Mighty One has done great things for me – holy is His name. His mercy extends to those who fear Him, from generation to generation.

LUKE 1:49-50 NIV

Fear the LORD, you His godly people, for those who fear Him will have all they need.

PSALM 34:9 NLT

"MY GRACE

IS SUFFICIENT

FOR YOU,

FOR MY

POWER IS

MADE PERFECT

IN WEAKNESS."

2 CORINTHIANS 12:9

A GOD OF GRACE

Some people focus so much on God's requirements and judgment, that they lose sight of His grace and compassion. He encourages you when the battle becomes too tough for you, He helps you up when you stumble or fall, and He shows you a better path when you make a mistake.

He wipes out the sins of the past and plans a better route for you to follow in the future. He wants to lead you and build you up to be spiritually strong. Since God is gracious and good to you, He expects you to be gracious and good to others.

God of love, help me to spread Your grace and peace to all I meet.

AMEN.

To each one of us grace has been given as Christ apportioned it.

EPHESIANS 4:7 NIV

Let us then approach God's throne of grace with confidence, so that we may receive mercy and find grace to help us in our time of need.

HEBREWS 4:16 NIV

God saved you by His grace when you believed. And you can't take credit for this; it is a gift from God.

EPHESIANS 2:8 NLT

God is able to make all grace abound to you, so that having all sufficiency in all things at all times, you may abound in every good work.

---

2 CORINTHIANS 9:8 ESV

Sin is no longer your master, for you no longer live under the requirements of the law. Instead, you live under the freedom of God's grace.

ROMANS 6:14 NLT

Through Him we have also obtained access by faith into this grace in which we stand, and we rejoice in hope of the glory of God.

ROMANS 5:2 ESV

From His abundance we have all received one gracious blessing after another.

JOHN 1:16 NLT

We praise God for the glorious grace He has poured out on us who belong to His dear Son.

EPHESIANS 1:6 NLT

For the grace of God has appeared, bringing salvation for all people.

TITUS 2:11 ESV

The God of all grace, who called you to His eternal glory in Christ, after you have suffered a little while, will Himself restore you and make you strong, firm and steadfast.

---

1 PETER 5:10 NIV

We are all saved the same way, by the undeserved grace of the Lord Jesus.

ACTS 15:11 NLT

I commend you to God and to the word of His grace, which is able to build you up and to give you the inheritance among all those who are sanctified.

ACTS 20:32 ESV

You know the generous grace of our Lord Jesus Christ. Though He was rich, yet for your sakes He became poor, so that by His poverty He could make you rich.

---

2 CORINTHIANS 8:9 NLT

May our Lord Jesus Christ Himself and God our Father, who loved us and by His grace gave us eternal encouragement and good hope, encourage your hearts and strengthen you in every good deed and word.

---

2 THESSALONIANS 2:16-17 NIV

May you experience the love of Christ, though it is too great to understand fully. Then you will be made complete with all the fullness of life and power that comes from God.

EPHESIANS 3:19 NLT

The LORD is compassionate and gracious, slow to anger, abounding in love.

PSALM 103:8 NIV

Even before I was born, God chose me and called me by His marvelous grace.

GALATIANS 1:15 NLT

The LORD will give grace and glory; no good thing will He withhold from those who walk uprightly.

PSALM 84:11 NKJV

Because of His grace He made us right in His sight and gave us confidence that we will inherit eternal life.

TITUS 3:7 NLT

If we walk
IN THE LIGHT,
as He
IS IN THE LIGHT,
we have
FELLOWSHIP
with one another,
AND THE BLOOD
OF JESUS, HIS SON,
CLEANSES US
FROM ALL SIN.
1 John 1:7

FELLOWSHIP
OF BELIEVERS

Christianity flourishes in fellowship, and sharing in Christian brotherhood is essential to spiritual growth. Do not neglect the fellowship of believers – it has great therapeutic value. Don't isolate yourself. Talk to others and ask for advice.

The early Christians also supported, taught and instructed one another. In this way they grew through the experience of fellowship with believers. Christians enrich themselves through fellowship with each other. This is what Jesus expects from us.

Holy Leader, thank You for the multitude of believers all over the world.

AMEN.

Let us think of ways to motivate one another to acts of love and good works. And let us not neglect our meeting together, as some people do, but encourage one another, especially now that the day of His return is drawing near.

HEBREWS 10:24-25 NLT

For as the body is one and has many members, but all the members of that one body, being many, are one body, so also is Christ.

---

1 CORINTHIANS 12:12 NKJV

This makes for harmony among the members, so that all the members care for each other. If one part suffers, all the parts suffer with it, and if one part is honored, all the parts are glad. All of you together are Christ's body, and each of you is a part of it.

---

1 CORINTHIANS 12:25-27 NLT

All the believers devoted themselves to the apostles' teaching, and to fellowship, and to sharing in meals (including the Lord's Supper), and to prayer.

ACTS 2:42 NLT

Be devoted to one another in love. Honor one another above yourselves.

ROMANS 12:10 NIV

Beloved, if God so loved us, we also ought to love one another.

---

1 JOHN 4:11 NKJV

We proclaim to you what we ourselves have actually seen and heard so that you may have fellowship with us. And our fellowship is with the Father and with His Son, Jesus Christ.

---

1 JOHN 1:3 NLT

If you have any encouragement from being united with Christ, if any comfort from His love, if any common sharing in the Spirit, if any tenderness and compassion, then make my joy complete by being like-minded, having the same love, being one in spirit and of one mind.

PHILIPPIANS 2:1-2 NIV

Be kind and compassionate to one another, forgiving each other, just as in Christ God forgave you.

EPHESIANS 4:32 NIV

Let no corrupting talk come out of your mouths, but only such as is good for building up, as fits the occasion, that it may give grace to those who hear.

EPHESIANS 4:29 ESV

Bear one another's burdens, and so fulfill the law of Christ.

GALATIANS 6:2 NKJV

Pay careful attention to your own work, for then you will get the satisfaction of a job well done, and you won't need to compare yourself to anyone else. For we are each responsible for our own conduct.

GALATIANS 6:4-5 NLT

"A new command I give you: Love one another. As I have loved you, so you must love one another. By this everyone will know that you are My disciples, if you love one another."

JOHN 13:34-35 NIV

Cheerfully share your home with those who need a meal or a place to stay.

1 PETER 4:9 NLT

Let the message of Christ dwell among you richly as you teach and admonish one another with all wisdom through psalms, hymns, and songs from the Spirit, singing to God with gratitude in your hearts.

COLOSSIANS 3:16 NIV

Let each of us please his neighbor for his good, to build him up.

ROMANS 15:2 ESV

"You are the salt of the earth. But what good is salt if it has lost its flavor? Can you make it salty again? It will be thrown out and trampled underfoot as worthless."

MATTHEW 5:13 NLT

"You are the light of the world. A town built on a hill cannot be hidden. Neither do people light a lamp and put it under a bowl. Instead they put it on its stand, and it gives light to everyone in the house. In the same way, let your light shine before others, that they may see your good deeds and glorify your Father in heaven."

MATTHEW 5:14-16 NIV

For you were once darkness, but now you are light in the Lord. Walk as children of light (for the fruit of the Spirit is in all goodness, righteousness, and truth).

EPHESIANS 5:8-9 NKJV

THE RIGHTEOUS

MAN

WALKS IN HIS

INTEGRITY;

HIS CHILDREN

ARE BLESSED

AFTER HIM.

PROVERBS 20:7

NOTES